A COMMENTARY ON

GALATIANS

A COMMENTARY ON

GALATIANS

Christ Plus Equals Nothing

TOM NETTLES
WITH SYLVIA NETTLES DICKSON

FREE
GRACE
PRESS

Published by

Free Grace Press
3900 Dave Ward Dr., Ste. 1900
Conway, AR 72034
(501) 214-9663
email: support@freegracepress.com
website: www.freegracepress.com

Printed in the United States of America

ISBN: 978-1-952599-40-8

Contents

Chapter 1

An Introduction

I. The Author of the Letter

There is very little contradiction, even from the most radical critics, that the apostle Paul wrote the letter to the Galatians. This was the "young man named Saul" who consented to Stephen's death and at whose feet the stoners of Stephen laid their robes (Acts 7:58–8:1). He was the one who was "ravaging the church" (8:3) and whose zeal did not allow him to relent in "breathing threats and murder against the disciples of the Lord" (9:1). He was the one Jesus threw to the ground by His glory and blinded and converted and called to become one of the suffering persecuted Christians (9:4–15). This is the new convert who debated and confounded the Jews as he demonstrated that Jesus was the Christ with such power that the Hellenistic Jews sought to kill him (9:22, 29).

Paul was taken by Barnabas from Tarsus to Antioch (9:30; 11:25, 26), a church that began with the conversion of the Hellenistic Jews, where disciples first were called Christians (11:20, 26). That church sent Barnabas and Saul to Jerusalem to carry relief to the believers there (11:29, 30). This church also sent them on mission, which carried them to Cyprus, to Antioch in Pisidia, and to Iconium, Lystra, and Derbe, cities in the southernmost part of Galatia. On this initial trip, Saul began to use the name Paul (Acts 13–14). We find him at the end of the book of Acts imprisoned at Rome but dwelling in his own rented house "teaching about the Lord Jesus Christ with all boldness and without hindrance" (28:30–31). It seems likely that he was released at this time from imprisonment in Rome since the charges against him were not convincing (26:31, 32), and went to Spain, sponsored by the Christians in Rome (Rom. 15:28). Upon returning, he again was imprisoned because of Nero's insane accusations against the Christians and soon was martyred at the hands of the Romans because of the opposition of the Jews, even as his Lord Himself (2 Tim. 4:6).

II. The Recipients of the Letter

Paul wrote this letter to churches in the region of Galatia, probably those he founded during his missionary journey with Barnabas in Acts 13 and 14, from which John Mark had departed (13:13). Opposition from Jews had been violent and almost led to Paul's death by stoning in Lystra (13:50; 14:2, 4, 5, 19). In Derbe and in the regions summarized so succinctly by Luke in Acts 14:21, Paul apparently suffered from the aftereffects of his severe stoning and was having great physical challenges and problems with his sight (Gal. 4:13–14). Before they returned to Antioch of Syria, they returned to Antioch of Pisidia and to Lystra and Iconium to strengthen the souls of the believers, exhort them to continue in the faith, and warn them that tribulations would come. Paul considered this return visit to be a part of his first visit to them (Gal. 4:13) and an illustration of what kind of persecution and physical suffering could come. God had saved him from death but was bringing to pass what he had promised at his commissioning as an apostle (Acts 9:15–16). Some have hypothesized that the northern portion of Galatia, composed of ethnic Galls, was the region where he had preached on another occasion to the churches to whom he wrote. The simplest answer to me points to that work narrated in Acts 13 and 14.

III. The Occasion of the Letter

Some supposedly believing Jews had come to these churches urging them to be circumcised. Why? First, to believe in the Jewish Messiah, they must be within the covenant community marked off by circumcision. The Messiah, in their view, came only to those who kept the covenant of Abraham (Gal. 3:17–18). Second, this would diminish the opposition that these Gentile believers had from the strong Jewish presence in those cities, as indicated by the earlier opposition to Paul. They could coexist on peaceable terms with the circumcision, still accepting the Messiah, if they too were circumcised. In this way they would "avoid being persecuted for the cross of Christ" (Gal. 5:11; 6:12 CSB). Paul saw this prompting by these Jewish teachers as a stark violation of the doctrines of the gospel as well as the call to discipleship. If in their heart they could be drawn to accept the views of the circumcision party, they would demonstrate that they had abandoned the way of acceptance before God as solely by the work of Christ (Gal. 5:2–4). Paul wrote this letter out of deep concern for their eternal welfare and in obedience to the reality that one must contend earnestly for the faith, for faith is not faith if it is not an immovable response to *the* faith.

IV. The Driving Theme of the Letter

The glory of Christ in His perfect obedience to all the requirements of the law is the driving theme of the epistle. Only Jesus Christ saves, for the life given through obedience to the law (Gal. 3:12) has been taken away by our corruption and personal disobedience. He alone has kept its every requirement in every nuance and implication, even suffering its curse, so that only union with Him by faith can set us right before God (2:16, 21; 3:10, 22; 4:4, 5; 5:4–6). If we seek to be justified by works, we are damned; if we come as sinners to the righteous crucified One, we will stand before God in His righteousness.

V. The Importance of the Letter

Though every item of revealed truth in this book is important and is to be valued as a heavenly jewel, two issues stand out as eminent in their importance. First, here we learn of the intensity with which we must cling to divine revelation as the only source of saving knowledge about God. This revelation has come through the apostles, was clear and completed within their corporate life-span, and continues to hold forth the truth of righteousness, forgiveness, and eternal life. These issues are never irrelevant and transcend the evanescent philosophies, deceitful values, and uncertainties that characterize the ever-shifting powers of this defiled age. Divine revelation is of infinite excellence, for it leads us to confess, embrace, and worship the one triune God in His unchanging and inexhaustible glory. Divine revelation captures the mind for eternal truth and not for the ever-changing guesses about life from fallen value-makers who do not want to retain God in their knowledge. Second, in this book we are confronted with the eternal beauty and virtuous power that is present in the moral law of God. Why all our righteousnesses are to be considered as filthy rags becomes clear in the constant refrain of our living under a curse. That righteousness can come to those who believe in Christ magnifies the poverty of our works and the infinite splendor of the completed work of Christ. By trusting in Him, we neither "overthrow the law" (Rom. 3:31), nor do we "nullify the grace of God" (Gal. 2:21).

Chapter 2

No Other Gospel

Galatians 1

I. A Quick but Pertinent Greeting (1:1–2)

A. Who Is Paul? (v. 1)

For the purpose of this letter, Paul identifies himself as an "apostle" (v. 1) The office of apostle was given to the church by Christ in the fullness of His authority as the conqueror of death and as exalted to the place of preeminence with the Father: "And he himself gave some to be apostles" (Eph. 4:11 CSB). The apostles received revelation concerning the new covenant, the person and work of Christ, justification, sanctification, final judgment, heaven, and hell. In addition, their instruction concerning the "good works" (Titus 3:8; see also Gal. 6:9, 10) that necessarily flow from salvation—as opposed to the "non-good works" (Eph. 2:9; Gal. 2:17; Titus 3:5) that dominate the unregenerate state—consists of revealed truth. Their word was inspired, authoritative, and final. It is important for the Galatians to see Paul as an apostle and not merely as a religious theoretician.

B. Who Commissioned Paul? (v. 1)

1. Paul's commission was not of human origin, and he did not answer to any human authority for his message. Unlike the false teachers, he did not have to please any religious court of human origin. Human authority or opinion in matters of gospel truth were of no consequence to Paul, for he had absolute confidence in the origin and the authority of the gospel he preached.

2. Paul's apostolic position was assigned to him specifically by Jesus Christ in accordance with the purpose of God the Father, "who raised him from the dead" (v. 1). The irrevocable character of his call is assured in that Jesus is raised from the dead, and this was done by the glory and according to the purpose of the Father (Rom. 6:4). For similar statements of Paul's unwavering confidence in his apostleship as an extension of the purpose of God as expressed in the resurrection of Christ, see Romans 1:1–6. "Through [Him] we have received grace and apostleship" (v. 5).

3. The immediacy of this apostolic call is seen in the undelayed activity in preaching the gospel and arguing for the messianic status of Jesus (Acts 9:19–22; 26–30). This persuasion is not diluted by his being commissioned along with Barnabas by the church at Antioch (Acts 13:1–3). Twice the text witnesses to

the sovereign work of the Holy Spirit in this commission (vv. 2, 4). This does demonstrate that even as an apostle Paul's work was an arm of ministry from the church and for the establishment and health of local churches. Apostles were among the body of gifts given to the body of Christ, the churches (Eph. 4:11–16).

C. Who Else Is Aware of This Letter? (v. 2)

As is often the case, Paul wrote the letter in the presence of other brothers (1 Cor. 16:20; 2 Cor. 13:13; Phil. 4:21; Col. 4:10–14). He had nothing to hide, and the things he wrote to the churches were for the spiritual good of all people. The brothers with him would offer no objection to the authority claimed by Paul and, therefore, would not dissent from his teaching.

D. To Whom Does He Send This Letter? (v. 2)

The letter was sent to some of the churches Paul and Barnabas had established in their ministry in Acts 14.

1. Paul experienced the extremes of human interaction in the context of his ministry in Lystra. Upon his healing of a lame man, they considered him a god, Hermes. The inhabitants, led by the pagan priests, rose to a height of piety in seeking to offer sacrifices to Barnabas and Paul (Acts 14:13). This act they considered piety, Paul condemned urgently and fervently as blasphemous idolatry (14:14–18). From a desire to worship these gospel missionaries, the people soon were persuaded to stone Paul with the intent of killing him (v. 19).

2. God's grace in the conversion of Gentiles more than compensated for the tribulations of the Galatian mission. Disciples were made in each of the cities they visited, and an example of faithfulness under pressure allowed the gospel preachers to exhort these disciples to continue in the faith with the admonition, "Through many tribulations we must enter the kingdom of God" (Acts 14:22).

3. The physical presence of the unbelieving Jews caused consistent interruption and opposition (Acts 14:4–5, 19) in this initial engagement of these churches with the gospel; now the doctrinal aberrations of the Judaizers stirred up an even more dangerous trouble—an amendment to the gospel to include works of righteousness based on ceremonial law.

4. When Paul received from the churches an offering for the church in Jerusalem, he noted again in authoritative language, "Now concerning the collection for the saints, as I directed the churches of Galatia, so you also are to do" (1 Cor. 16:1). While Paul sought to persuade the churches to give expression to their love for the brethren from deeply ingrained spiritual motives, he did hesitate as an apostle to order the churches to specific courses of action.

Sylvia's Comments (1:1–2)

When Paul introduces this letter, I get the impression that he is not just using "apostle" as a title but reestablishing his authority to speak. He emphasizes it is God who gave him the authority and no one else. He's speaking also with "all the brothers" supporting this letter. Furthermore, he states that he's not speaking from his past respected position in Judaism. His trust is not in what other people think of him or the wisdom of man but in God the Father and the resurrected Christ. This letter is to the churches in Galatia, which is in the southern part of present-day Turkey.

II. An Intense and Pertinent Benediction (1:3–5)

A. Pointing to Blessings from God (v. 3)

Paul points the Galatians to the covenantal blessings of grace and peace. None of the blessings of this covenant are merited by the recipients, but all flow from grace, an eternal propensity in God to manifest His goodness by bringing His enemies into a state of infinite blessedness. For this to be done, a state of peace must be accomplished by a commensurate act of reconciliation, a gift provided by the offended one and not by the offenders, even in opposition to the moral stance of those for whom the blessing is designed. Grace operates, therefore, through peace, and both mercy and justice are satisfied.

1. The covenant of grace concerns the particular purpose of God to save sinners by His operations of grace through the work of His Son. This is an eternal covenant with particular individuals made through and included in Christ as the One through whose gracious condescension they will be saved. This gracious arrangement made by the triune God in eternity forms the basis of his argument that the

temporary measures of ceremonial have been fulfilled and thus rendered inoperative by the completed work of Christ. To this abiding principle Paul refers frequently as in this reminder to Timothy: "Who saved us and called us to a holy calling, not because of our works but because of his own purpose and grace, which he gave us in Christ Jesus before the ages began, and which now has been manifested through the appearing of our Savior Christ Jesus, who abolished death and brought life and immortality to light through the gospel" (2 Tim. 1:9, 10).

2. Isaiah 54:10 speaks of the arrangement for salvation as a covenant of peace: "For the mountains may depart and the hills be removed, but my steadfast love shall not depart from you, and my covenant of peace shall not be removed." This passage refers to the provision of peace, reconciliation, established by eternal covenant as a vial element of the atoning work of Christ, a specific blessing Paul has in mind in the passage in Colossians: "And you, who once were alienated and hostile in mind, doing evil deeds, he has now reconciled in his body of flesh by his death, in order to present you holy and blameless and above reproach before him" (Col. 1:21–22). It also refers to the abolishing of the separation the ceremonial law made between Jew and Gentile so that those who did not have the "covenants of promise" and were "far off" have been "brought near by the blood of Christ. For he himself is our peace, who has made both one, and has broken down the dividing wall of hostility" (Eph. 2:12–14). It is precisely the "dividing wall of

hostility" in the ceremonial law that the false teachers Paul opposes are seeking to reconstruct in arguing for the necessity of circumcision.

B. The Son's Part in the Covenant (vv. 3–4)

In this covenant of grace and peace, what did the Son pledge to do for the people given to Him?

1. He gave *Himself.* His death was voluntary. This gift to sinners was resident within the secret and eternal counsels of God. For eternity the Son finds His unchanging joy by His submission to the provision of the covenant of redemption manifest in the covenant of grace and the covenant of peace, according to which He laid down His life. "For this reason the Father loves me, because I lay down my life that I may take it up again. No one takes it from me, but I lay it down of my own accord. I have authority to lay it down, and I have authority to take it up again. This charge I have received from my Father" (John 10:17–18).

2. He gave Himself *for our sins.* His death was substitutionary. He died in the stead of the people the Father had given Him. "I lay down my life for the sheep" (John 10:15). "For their sake I consecrate myself [set myself apart as a sacrifice], that they also may be sanctified in truth" (John 17:19).

3. He gave Himself "for our sins to deliver us from the present evil age" (v. 4).

   - The physical world is fallen and groaning, awaiting the revelation of the sons of God and their glorification (Rom. 8:19), and then it will be delivered from its captivity to corruption.

- The moral texture of this age—all the years after the fall and prior to the return of the Redeemer—is destructive to all that is noble and reminiscent of the image of God; the redeemed are being reconstituted in that image (Gal. 4:6, 7; 5:24–26; Eph. 4:20–24).

- The wrath of God will eternally consume those who remain in ungodliness, but the reconciled are accordingly rescued from the just retribution that is to come on "the present evil age." In service of that grace—justification before God in the day of retribution—Paul writes this letter.

C. The Will of Our God and Father (v. 4)

What is the significance of the "will of our God and Father" in verse 4?

1. As there is only a single will in the one true God, there is also a particular way in which that will is eternally known and expressed by each person of the Trinity (John 10:27–30).

2. The Father has a will for the Son and is conscious of the Son's obedience to that will (John 10:15, 17; Phil. 2:8–11).

3. The Son knows the Father's will and, as the Son, wills the same thing in a manner fitting for the Son so that He carries out the divine will as the Son of obedience (John 5:30; 8:38; 10:37–38).

4. The Son did not gain redemption only according to His own will and then induce the Father to save the people for whom He died. He died for them in accordance with the Father's desire to save them (John 6:37–40).

D. The Resulting Manifestation of His Glory (v. 5)

How does this arrangement result in the manifestation of His glory "forever and ever"?

1. As the Father is glorified for the manifestation of His attributes in this eternal covenant (Eph. 1:6), so is each person of the triune God glorified in relation to the completion of the provisions of this covenant (Eph. 1:12, 14).

2. The glory of this manifestation truly is infinite, and each person of the Godhead shares in this infinite glory.

3. If one may use the language about eternity, it "originates" in the electing prerogative of the Father and each person of the Trinity demonstrates infinite love according to the particular operations of each in this covenant of grace (2 Cor. 13:14).

4. This is the very purpose of creation—the full manifestation of the divine attributes. Redemption displays holiness, righteousness, justice, immutability, patience, lovingkindness, mercy, and eventually, as the redeemed shall see, all the other manifest facets of the singularly glorious triune God.

Sylvia's Comments (vv. 3–5)

After this reintroduction, Paul, in his typical way, speaks of grace, peace, and glory. His focus is to bring glory to God and remind the Galatians of who they are. Christ and the Father are still actively giving grace and peace. The Galatians' times are evil, as are ours, and sometimes we all forget who is in charge. They—as well as all believers—have been delivered "from the present evil age." What a magnificent place to be. Remember, Christ taught us to pray, "Lead us not into temptation, but deliver us from evil" (Matt. 6:13). Here we have it: we have been delivered through Christ's sacrifice. God set it up. God did it. We don't need to worry about our place in Him through faith in Christ. We can shout out, "God, you are glorious all the time!"

Yes, we still live in this present evil age with temptation and evil around us. Nothing, however, that happens now can separate us, sweep us away, condemn us, or enslave us again (Rom. 8:38–39). It's good to be reminded of this when the world spins chaotically in personal, political, economic, and even religious circles.

III. A Confrontive and Pertinent Engagement with the Issue (1:6–10)

A. *Paul Is Astonished (v. 6)*

In verse 6, Paul tells the Galatians he is astonished. What constitutes this astonishment?

1. This departure of gospel truth happened so quickly. Paul and Barnabas had been with them and taught them thoroughly with powerful clarity (see 3:1) and a display of apostolic gifts (see 3:5). What sort of persuasion would make them forget the power and clarity of that time of ministry?

2. Their shift takes them away from the one true God, that is, "him who called you." If they find another message more compelling, they are leaving the one true God, for it is He Himself who gives the call to salvation through the gospel.

3. Their new persuasion reflects on their evaluation of the worthiness of Christ Himself: "deserting him who called you in the grace of Christ" for the sake of a teaching that undercuts the all-sufficiency of Christ (2:16; 3:13–14, 24–26). God the Father saves sinners through no one but Christ, for He only is qualified to save, and He only has done the saving work.

4. That particular aspect of Christ's work is called the "grace of Christ." Paul here refers to the aspect of its freeness, for all the work of meriting eternal life has been done by Christ. He is not referring to the gracious change of heart brought about by the regenerating power of the Holy Spirit, for none can fall from that. But he argues that they are substituting a salvation partly produced by Christ and partly by their own obedience. They have forsaken the teaching of grace. He refers to this again in 5:4–5: "You are severed from Christ, you who would be justified by the law; you have fallen away from grace. For through the Spirit, by faith, we ourselves eagerly wait

for the hope of righteousness." Instead of receiving and maintaining a teaching of grace, they receive a teaching of ceremonial works.

5. The content promulgated by these other teachers as the gospel is demonstrably not what Paul taught. It is a "different gospel." Either they are right and Paul is wrong, or Paul is right and they are wrong. There is no way of synthesizing these two messages.

B. Some Teachers Distort the Gospel (v. 7)

1. Though Paul called this delusion a different "gospel," he reminded the Galatians that the true gospel is exclusive of any other way of being justified before God. "Another" gospel is no gospel at all.

2. For the sake of their personal gain, these teachers were disturbing the churches of Galatia. They followed in the wake of Paul and sought to undo his message, for they themselves did not grasp the offense of the cross. Christ crucified is a stumbling block to the Jews (1 Cor. 1:22–23). That God would grant salvation even to those who have not obeyed the ceremonial law, at least to some external measure, was inconceivable to these agitators.

Sylvia's Comments (vv. 6–7)

Now Paul really gets to the meat of the letter. He's perplexed, puzzled, exasperated that they are listening to false teachers. These people are saying theirs is the true gospel, which is different from the one Paul introduced. He points out that they are not deserting Paul but God, who poured out grace and the faith to be redeemed by the work of Christ.

Are we easily led astray by pleasant-sounding doctrines that have a false ring? Do we let them lull us with their soft chiming and mellow tones? James tells us to seek wisdom from above in faith, and God will give it to us. We have more than the Galatians had to guide them. We have the complete Scripture full of God's wisdom to guide us. Therefore, look there and examine what is true, right, pure, etc., as spoken in Philippians 4:8.

C. Only One Gospel (vv. 8–9)

Distortion of the gospel is a damning proposition. Paul gives a breathtaking explosion of confidence in the absolute truthfulness of the gospel that he preached to them.

1. First, he includes himself as a possible gospel felon should he shift his message and preach something different from what he had already preached. He knew he was under the inspiration and revelatory work of the Spirit in that preaching, and should he now turn to a different scheme of redemption, this new message of his should be rejected.

2. Second, he entertained the startling idea that an angel from heaven, not a fallen angel already assigned to hell, might appear to seek to correct Paul's message with something claiming to come from the throne of God Himself. Paul warns them not to be deceived by this. The only saving message present among men is "the one we preached to you." That is the message

they had received, and that alone is the saving truth of the gospel.

3. Paul pronounces an anathema on any being at all who would change what he preached: "Let him be accursed!" Any such perversion of truth is really from hell and is spoken by those whose proper abode is hell. If they so deceive as to minimize Christ in His saving work, if they want to insert human conformity to mere types and shadows as sharing the glory of salvation with Christ, then they themselves are yet in their sins, still under condemnation and bound for an eternal home of unrelenting wrath from God. That they seek to lead others with them makes them doubly damned.

D. Whose Approval Does Paul Seek? (v. 10)

Paul does not seek men's approval. He only desires to prove himself a faithful steward. While they accuse him of courting popularity by easing the requirements for the Gentiles in letting them sidestep the ceremonial law, Paul looked upon them as avoiding persecution "for the cross of Christ" (6:12). Paul, however, did not care for the opinion of men in this matter but only the truth of the gospel. He asked them, therefore, if his language seemed like the language of a man-pleaser. The only way he could do any good for man was to tell the truth. The only way he could be faithful to his calling was to tell the truth. The only way he could honor God was to tell the truth. The only way for sin to be forgiven and eternal life to be granted was to preach this truth, his gospel.

Sylvia's Comments (vv. 8–10)

Paul is so passionate about this and so assured that he is right, he calls for anyone or anything that trades the true gospel for a false, or even tainted, one to be cursed. This cursing is not just a way of saying, "Don't listen to this garbage," but rather, to hold these liars fully accountable for their treachery. He calls for a public denouncing of them and turning them out of the fellowship of believers, leaving their eternal fate in God's hands. With that, he challenges the gossip these people have spread about him. False rumors must have been circulating, saying he only wanted attention and glory for himself. I imagine these liars were trying to discredit Paul and the other apostles so they could garner the trust, recognition, and gain they sought.

IV. Why Paul Is So Sure of His Position (1:11–12)

Paul is adamantly sure of his position because of who gave it to him.

A. A Gospel Not Taught by Man (vv. 11–12)

Paul's gospel was not a thing he was taught by man. Paul expressed confidence throughout his ministry that his preaching did not arise from any human philosophy or moral system. He wrote to the Thessalonians, "But just as we have been approved by God to be entrusted with the gospel, so we speak, not to please man, but to please God who tests our hearts" (1 Thess. 2:4).

B. A Gospel from Christ (v. 12)

Paul's gospel came ("I received it") through "a revelation of Jesus Christ"—that is, from Christ and about Christ.

1. Christ confronted him on the road to Damascus (Acts 9:3–6). "Who are you, Lord? . . . I am Jesus, whom you are persecuting" (9:5)

2. Christ shone in his heart "to give the light of the knowledge of the glory of God in the face of Jesus Christ" (2 Cor. 4:6). Paul received both propositional revelation in explanation of Christ's person and his work of salvation; also, he had the sensible impression of the awe-inspiring holy beauty of God as manifest in Christ shed abroad in his heart by the Holy Spirit (Rom. 5:5).

3. His message after this confrontation from Christ was about Jesus as the Christ. "Immediately he proclaimed Jesus in the synagogues, saying, 'He is the Son of God.' . . . Saul increased all the more in strength, and confounded the Jews who lived in Damascus by proving that Jesus was the Christ" (Acts 9:20, 22).

4. The revelation included a revelation of Christ to Paul (Gal. 1:16) in which he saw the glory of Christ's person, the necessity and fullness of His atoning work, and the glory of His resurrection, ascension, and coming again in glory. All these marvelous details about Christ and His lordship and His relation to our salvation, resurrection, judgment, and eternal future were included in this revelation of Christ to Paul. Paul points to revelation as superior to deductions drawn from empiricism and reason: "'What no eye has seen,

nor ear heard, nor the heart of man imagined, what God has prepared for those who love him'—these things God has revealed to us through the Spirit" (1 Cor. 2:9–10, see also verses 6–13). Ephesians 3:1–7 focuses on the reception of revelation of the mystery: "How the mystery was made known to me by revelation . . . which was not made known to the sons of men in other generations as it has now been revealed to his holy apostles and prophets by the Spirit" (verses 3, 5). These verses give specific information about the fullness and glory of the revelation Paul received. Some revelations given to him had such overwhelming glory that imparting their content in words was impossible (2 Cor. 12:1–6).

Sylvia's Comments (vv. 11–12)

I love what Paul says here: he calls them brothers. It's kind of like he took a breath and refocused on what binds them together. Now, he could be gearing up for the next part, but I hear him using a gentler tone. He is restating what he said earlier—the gospel he preached to them came by a revelation from Christ, not from anyone else, including the other apostles.

V. Historical Evidence of Paul's Apostleship (1:13–24)

A. A Zealous Persecutor (vv. 13-14, 23-24)

Paul experienced a radical change of perspective from rabid opponent to unswerving advocate of the gospel of

Jesus Christ. He was a zealous and learned persecutor of the church and became a preacher, promoter, and sufferer for the message he had once opposed and hated.

1. Saul—his pre-Christian, pre-apostolic name (Acts 8:1; 9:22; 13:1, 9—took part in the stoning of Stephen, and apparently his approval to this action was a major element of its prosecution (Acts 7:58; 8:1). It led to a systematic and aggressive attempt to eliminate all who confessed that Jesus of Nazareth was the Christ (Acts 8:3; 9:1–2).

2. Ananias was called by the Lord to set the persecutor apart as an apostle to the "Gentiles and kings and the children of Israel" (Acts 9:15). Ananias seemed alarmed at seeking Paul out, for he had heard "from many about this man, how much evil he has done to your saints at Jerusalem" (Acts 9:13).

3. Immediately upon Paul's first occasion of gospel preaching in Damascus, the question circulated with amazement, "Is not this the man who made havoc in Jerusalem of those who called upon this name? And has he not come here for this purpose?" (Acts 9:21).

4. The saints in Judea, who had received the greatest blow from Saul of Tarsus in his zeal against the church, heard that he had changed: "He who used to persecute us is now preaching the faith he once tried to destroy" (Gal. 1:23).

B. A Zealous Pharisee (v. 14)

Paul's zeal for the "traditions of my fathers" would not have been overthrown by anything less than an irrefutable demonstration that his views were incorrect.

1. Paul had far outstripped his peers in knowledge of Scripture interpreted through the traditions of the scribes.

   - He was convinced that the lowliness of Jesus of Nazareth, His rejection by the chief teachers and rabbinic scholars, His crucifixion at the hands of Gentiles, and His reception of the "scum"—the traitors and the sinners among the sons and daughters of Abraham—eliminated any possibility that He could be the Messiah. Samaritans and Gentiles also partook of His teaching and His compassion. Blasphemous, therefore, were the claims that He was the long-expected Messiah and the fulfiller of the covenantal promises of Yahweh to Abraham and David and the One who would make all His enemies a footstool for His feet. For this mode of messianic interpretation, Paul was "extremely zealous."

   - The extremity of his zeal and his knowledge of the Old Testament, though misapplied, served as preparation for the work he immediately would do upon the change in his orientation to Jesus of Nazareth. Intensity of hatred and outrage for what he believed a falsehood was transformed into a greater sense of joy and worship when he found that Jesus was indeed the Christ.

2. The superiority of the gospel message to all he had believed before transformed his outlook. He counted all supposed personal advantages of pedigree and assumed personal righteousness as loss because of the

surpassing excellency of Jesus Christ (Phil. 3:8–9). Had he held on to these things, he would have lost his life under the judgment of God forever. These trinkets of personal gain were indeed less than nothing—not merely neutral but damning. He calculated the relation of his accumulations of applause from his peers and counted them as rubbish in comparison to the true worthiness of Christ.

C. An Immediate Change (vv. 15–16)

Paul changed immediately to embrace Jesus as the One who came to reign as Messiah.

He listed in chronological order the saving action of God toward him: "But when he who had set me apart before I was born, and who called me by his grace, was pleased to reveal his Son to me, in order that I might preach him among the Gentiles, I did not immediately consult with anyone." The intensity of Paul's sense of purpose forms an element of his defense of his true apostleship and thus of the inviolability of the message he preached.

1. All the events of Paul's life proceeded according to the divine pleasure. In Ephesians 1:5, Paul wraps up the entirety of the blessings the Father grants to the elect in Christ in His "good pleasure" (NKJV). Now he makes it specific to his own call to salvation and his preaching ministry of the gospel, a ministry designed specifically to reach even to the Gentiles.

2. This pleasure of God toward Paul already was operating as Paul was in his mother's womb, and at his

birth he was moving toward the consummation, in God's own time, of this special design for the one who would say, "For to me to live is Christ, and to die is gain" (Phil. 1:21). The determination for Paul's apostleship was an element of the means conceived for the execution of the covenant of redemption but began its historical manifestation when he was physically conceived.

3. At the proper time, according to God's determination, Paul was called by grace. Grace was present already in the decrees of eternity but began its existential operation in Paul's spiritual perceptions when he saw Christ on the Damascus Road: "Lord, what do You want me to do?" (Acts 9:6 NKJV). Though Christ's glorious appearance was physically blinding, it was spiritually enlightening: "God . . . has shone in our hearts to give the light of the knowledge of the glory of God in the face of Jesus Christ" (2 Cor. 4:6). Effectual calling is described in the Westminster Shorter Catechism (Q31) as "the work of God's Spirit, whereby, convincing us of our sin and misery, enlightening our minds in the knowledge of Christ, and renewing our wills, he doth persuade and enable us to embrace Jesus Christ freely offered us in the gospel."

4. Paul not only required internal enlightening of the glory of Christ for conversion but also the cognitive, propositional revelation of the person of Christ and the details of the nature of His redemptive work. As he testified in 1 Corinthians 2, "these things God has revealed to us through the Spirit . . . that we might understand the things freely given us by God" (verses

10, 12). Paul gave unwavering assurance that "by revelation He made known to me the . . . mystery of Christ, . . . which in other ages was not made known to the sons of men, as it has now been revealed by the Spirit to His holy apostles and prophets" (Eph. 3:3–5 NKJV). All the knowledge of the Messiah that Paul had absorbed and codified in his personal reading and formal education now underwent a revolutionary alteration. The contents of Christ's life that had been so off-putting to Saul of Tarsus now became the central facts that specified the messianic lordship of Jesus. Not through a restoration of the kingdom to Israel would the Messiah reign but through ushering in a complete and compelling righteousness in His own life, death, resurrection, and ascension. Messianic credentials lay not in the fulfillment of the political expectations of an earthly kingdom without redemption. The Messiah must be a sin-bearer before He could be a crown-wearer. The exclusivity of a people distinguished by certain ceremonies and sacrifices must give way to the particularity of a people set apart for forgiveness of sins, producing zeal for truly good works.

5. This revolution of content through revelatory truth led to the particular work of preaching Christ among the Gentiles (v. 16). The testimony was consistent:

- "To me, though I am the very least of all the saints, this grace was given, to preach to the Gentiles the unsearchable riches of Christ" (Eph. 3:8).

- "Of which I became a minister according to the stewardship from God that was given to me for you, to make the word of God fully known, the mystery hidden for ages and generations but now revealed to his saints. To them God chose to make known how great among the Gentiles" (Col. 1:25–27).

- "The man Christ Jesus, who gave himself as a ransom for all, which is the testimony given at the proper time. For this I was appointed a preacher and an apostle (I am telling the truth, I am not lying), a teacher of the Gentiles in faith and truth" (1 Tim. 2:5–7).

To the Galatian churches, therefore, the apostle was appointed specifically by God to bring them to a pure and sound faith by his preaching of the truth received through the revelation of Christ.

Sylvia's Comments (vv. 13–17)

Paul admits openly who he was before his conversion, something they already knew. He fought against the church and plotted to destroy it. He was a big deal—the real thing. His passion for Judaism exceeded everything else so that he was solely focused on annihilating these followers of Jesus, whom he saw as wanting to destroy the Jewish traditions, beliefs, and way of life. But God had other plans. God set him apart, called him by His grace, and revealed His Son so that he could go to the Gentiles. (Can you imagine being a devout Jew and going to the Gentiles? Only God could design that!) Paul's amazing conversion came solely from his encounter with the risen Christ. What a breathtaking occurrence, that Saul, the protector and defender of Judaism and persecutor of Christians, would be directly confronted by Jesus, the Messiah, stopped in his tracks, turned completely around, and remade into a spokesman to the Gentiles.

D. A Direct Revelation from Christ (vv. 16–22)

Paul proves he did not receive this message from the other apostles but had direct apostolic revelation as his only instructor in these matters of Christ and His cross. He did not consult with "flesh and blood" (v. 16 NKJV), meaning the instruction of the other apostles concerning the doctrines of the gospel. The demonstration of the truth of this claim is important for the spiritual health of the Galatian churches. He does this by referring to his personal history in relation to the apostles. This brief biographical vignette is set within the context of Acts 9:22–30.

1. In Acts 9:22, Paul's strength of presentation confounded the Jews who debated him concerning the relation of the man Jesus of Nazareth to the profile of the Messiah in the Old Testament. These gospel presentations in the face of highly learned opposition came without consultation with any who knew the gospel before him (Gal. 1:17). He did a brief personal evangelistic mission in Arabia and then returned to Damascus, where the Jews, entirely aggravated with their inability to overcome the exegetical prowess of Paul, made plans to kill him.

2. "After three years" (v. 18)—that is, three years from the time of his appointment to preach—he went to Jerusalem for a two-week visit with Peter. He also spoke with James, the brother of Jesus. Paul

emphasizes the certainty and truthfulness of this chronology and its implications of his independent knowledge of the gospel by making a solemn oath before God of its absolute conformity to reality (v. 20).

3. Near this time, Paul had a second visit to Jerusalem where he met the other apostles through the mediating spirit of the Son of Consolation, Barnabas (Acts 9:26–28). On this occasion, his preaching was so bold and strong that another plot was hatched against his life. The brothers in Jerusalem sent him away, therefore, and eventually he returned to Tarsus. He refers to this in the simple sentence, "Then I went into the regions of Syria and Cilicia" (Gal. 1:21). Outside of Jerusalem, he still was "unknown in person to the churches of Judea that are in Christ" (v. 22).

Sylvia's Comments (vv. 18–24)

After being with Ananias in Damascus, Paul didn't discuss this with anyone, including the other apostles. It was three years later when he spent time with Peter and James. He knows this is hard to believe, so he vows before God it is the truth. This is a strong statement for him to make. They should believe him based on their own relationship with him, but he stakes his claims with absolute security on God. Then he picks up again with his travel itinerary and points out that the Judean churches still didn't know him. They heard stories and good reports that brought praises of God to their lips, but they personally had not met nor heard him—there were no YouTube or video chats in those days.

E. Paul's Authority Firmly Established

We find in this chapter a greeting saturated with Paul's assertion of authority combined with a brief but tight presentation of the gospel he preached.

Paul then begins the presentation of the historical evidence for his independence in having received an apostolic commission and a revelation of the gospel from God Himself. Are we to believe Paul? Should we conclude that not only is he in dead earnest but also is neither deceived nor deceitful? If we surrender the certainty, clarity, sufficiency, and finality of Paul's gospel, we surrender the truth and eternal life.

Chapter 3

Sinners Need to Be Justified

Galatians 2

I. Historical Evidence Presented (2:1–10)

Paul continues to demonstrate the authenticity of his gospel through historical narrative. His description of this event and its historical importance in dealing with the relation of the Gentiles—and consequently all Christians—to the ceremonial law, shows the relentless attempts of the Judaizers to corrupt the gospel and Paul's more relentless pursuit of gospel clarity and purity.

A. Paul's Reason for Visiting the Other Apostles (vv. 1–2)

In verses 1–10, Paul describes an event that occurred

fourteen years after his first visit with Peter and James. This visit is described in Acts 15:1–2 and then throughout the rest of the Galatians 2.

1. His friend and defender, Barnabas, the Son of Encouragement, co-laborer in the mission to the Gentiles, went with him to Jerusalem, as did the Gentile Titus. Titus is not mentioned in the Acts account, perhaps because he was Luke's brother. Titus's presence was an important point for Paul's historical argument.

2. He went because of "a revelation" (v. 2). God told Paul to go for the controversy was yet in the future and the way was prepared by this journey for Paul's extended historical defense of his personal conduct and preaching among the Gentiles.

3. When he arrived, those who "seemed to be influential," or "of reputation" (v. 2 NASB95), requested a private meeting with Paul to hear him out (Acts 15:4–5). This meeting occurred in private because the Jerusalem group, in light of the strong advocates of Mosaic ceremony still resident in the church, wanted to make sure of the purity of his message and that he grasped the delicate nature of some of the issues involved.

4. Paul had no fear of having "run in vain" (v. 2). On his way to this meeting, he elicited great joy among believers in Samaria and Phoenicia by describing the conversion of the Gentiles. The fear was among the Jerusalem group because it included "some of the sect of the Pharisees who believed" (Acts 15:5 NKJV). In recounting this to the Galatians, Paul called them

"false brothers" (Gal. 2:4). They were the ones who brought fear and caution into the discussion. The apostles wanted to make sure that Paul was not a reactionary, having gone beyond the clearly revealed truth of the gospel into some kind of cultural reaction against Judaism. We find that throughout Paul's ministry, he carefully maintained the foundation of revelatory truth in the Old Testament and the promises that came through the nation of Israel (Acts 24:10–16; Rom. 1:1–3; 4:1–12; 9:1–8; 11:1–36; Gal. 3:15–22, et al.).

5. They had this caution because of the influence of the false brothers to whom Paul referred in verse 4. The exact place of these false brothers is not quite clear. The account in Acts says that they "rose up" to defend the continuation of circumcision. Paul seems to indicate that some made their way into the closed meeting to influence the outcome of the evaluation of Paul's doctrine preached to the Gentiles.

Sylvia's Comments (vv. 1–2)

Paul continues his timeline with his going back to Jerusalem fourteen years later with Barnabas and Titus. He went because God prompted him to go through a revelation. This seems to be a verification process for both the Jerusalem leaders and Paul. God sent him there to establish human witnesses to what he was teaching and preaching. They probably searched the Scriptures together to affirm solidly the Gentile ministry and conversions.

B. A Gospel Received by Revelation (vv. 3-10)

Paul points to evidence from this visit that he received his gospel by revelation:

1. Titus was not circumcised even though Judaizers were present in the Jerusalem congregation.

   - Despite this caution and even the presence of the ceremonial absolutists, Titus, a Greek convert, was not compelled to be circumcised. Had the "false brothers," the ostensibly believing Pharisees, been able to influence the outcome, one may legitimately wonder if the gospel as we know it would have survived beyond this interview. A divided apostolic witness would invalidate any claim to absolute truth concerning God's way of reconciling sinners.

   - Sometimes controversies may appear to be tempests in teapots to many observers, but to those who see the long-term implications, they become essential elements of faithful discipleship.

2. I call these stealthy intruders "ceremonial absolutists" because they conflated the ceremonial law with the moral law.

   - They gave Old Testament ceremonies the status of moral oughtness, contending that none were candidates for salvation through the Jewish Messiah who would not submit to Jewish ceremonies. Paul makes clear distinctions between ceremonial law and moral law in this letter. If one would seek to impose the one (that is, the lesser) as essential, then how much more must one impose the other (that is, the greater) as constituting righteousness. But the latter, the moral law, does not communicate righteousness to us but places us under a curse (Gal. 3:10; 5:3).

- Paul demonstrates the spirituality of the moral law and how its claim on our conduct is made manifest in the work of the Spirit in molding our character according to its mandates (Gal. 5:14–18, 22–23). True spirituality, true conformity to the character of God consists of the sanctifying influences of the Spirit in granting a joyful conformity to the revealed prerogatives of God in the moral law. If we would know how to worship God and give Him glory and how to honor His image-bearers in a fitting way, we will find it in the moral law expressed in the Ten Commandments.

- In addition, he demonstrates that condemnation comes from a life of disobedience to the moral law (5:20–21). This disobedience permeates the attitudes and actions of the unrepentant so that their final destination is eternal condemnation. The violations of the first table of the commandments are summarized in the words *idolatry* and *sorcery*. The violations of the second table reflect the inventive energy of the godless mind in finding ways to be consumed in pleasure-seeking self-centeredness and destructive attitudes toward neighbors.

3. Those who were of "high reputation" did not see fit to alter Paul's message and practice in any way. He stood his ground against the Judaizers (v. 5) even though his resistance to them could be misinterpreted. For

the sake of the Gentiles and the purity of the gospel, Paul saw through their subtlety and did not allow any dilution of the gospel of pure grace so "that the truth of the gospel might continue with you" (v. 5 NKJV).

Sylvia's Comments (vv. 3–6)

In verse 3, we are given a glimpse of part of the Galatian controversy—circumcision. No one at the Jerusalem meeting saw a need to submit the Gentiles to the law, represented here by circumcision. Yielding to the "brothers" requiring circumcision would take away the freedom of Christ in the gospel. Submitting to anything outside of justification by faith means putting ourselves back in slavery and corrupting the witness of the gospel. The leaders in Jerusalem did not require Paul or the other leaders in the Gentile church to add in any aspect of the law.

---

4. The pillars of the Jerusalem church saw Paul's message as authentic and the same that Peter had preached to the "circumcision" (vv. 6–8).

- Though having begun their ministry of preaching the gospel in different places, at different times, and without any discussion or comparison, they preached the same gospel. Given the startling manner of how God fulfilled the prophecies and the entirety of the law in the person and work of Christ, this lack of any inconsistency or contradiction is amazing and reaches the level of the proof of a common origin—the very mind and purpose of God revealed to human vessels chosen by God for the purpose.

- In addition, the powerful operations of God's Spirit among the Gentiles were parallel to that among the Jews under Peter's preaching. "For he who worked through Peter for his apostolic ministry to the circumcised worked also through me for mine to the Gentiles" (v. 8). Note, on this point, the words of Paul to the Thessalonian church: "Our gospel came to you not only in word, but also in power and in the Holy Spirit and with full conviction" (1 Thess. 1:5).

5. In an act of fraternal confidence, the pillars of Jerusalem gave Paul and Barnabas the "right hand of fellowship" (v. 9), a sort of commissioning of them as having special work among the Gentiles. The unity of Jew and Gentile in the gospel also would be manifest in the care that the Gentiles would show to those suffering on account of the gospel in Jerusalem. Paul and Barnabas were eager to demonstrate this unity—having one gospel, they also had one heart (Rom. 15:7–9; 2 Cor. 8:8–15; 9:10–15).

Sylvia's Comments (vv. 7–10)

Peter, James, and John (and maybe others) were involved in the discussions with Paul. Everyone agreed that God had made Paul an apostle to take the gospel to the uncircumcised. In the same manner, Peter was declared an apostle to the circumcised. God the Spirit was at work in both areas of ministry. I can picture this solemn meeting breaking into joyful praise and hugs all around as they excitedly responded to God's grace poured out freely, abundantly, and happily. This addendum to remember the poor was not an afterthought but a point that bound both Gentiles and Jews—all are needy in some way. Spiritual poverty is overcome through Christ, and Christ's church should be the first to respond to the material needs of its members and others.

II. A Painful but Authenticating Confrontation (2:11–14)

Though Paul would not desire such an event as this, and he has no desire or delight in invoking the inconsistency of Peter, in God's providence it provided an airtight example of Paul's argument for the absoluteness of the gospel as he had preached it to the Galatians. What he said to Peter, he would say to all who would amend the gospel message by word or conduct.

A. Peter's Hypocrisy Influences Others (vv. 11–13)

Though Peter had stood strong in the context of Jerusalem in the company of his fellow leaders of the church in Jerusalem, a later event made him panic under pressure and give the impression that he still considered the Gentiles unclean. As he ate with Gentiles, lo and behold, some pretenders at Christianity came from Jerusalem (vv. 11–13). With Peter leading the way, Barnabas and even the rest of the Jews present at the meal separated themselves from their proximity to the Gentiles, as if they were to maintain those nationalistic and ethnic practices built on the ceremonial distinctions between Jew and Gentile. The amazing power of social acceptance has its most disarming illustration in this event.

1. Peter had experienced an elongated lesson from heaven about not considering non-Jews as unclean (Acts 10:9–16). As a result of the revelation and the voice from heaven, he had gone to the house of a Gentile to preach the gospel. In the process of introducing his subject he noted, "Truly I understand that God shows no partiality, but in every nation anyone who fears him and does what is right is acceptable to him" (Acts 10:34–35). Now, however, "fearing the circumcision party" (Gal. 2:12), he withdrew from those accepted by God through the gospel in order not to offend the self-important, pseudo-believers from among the Pharisees. Fear may help avoid danger, but it can just as easily destroy a conscience.

2. How could it be! Barnabas, the defender of the newly converted Saul of Tarsus (Acts 9:27) and co-laborer in the initial extended mission to the Gentiles (Acts 13:2–3), sensed danger in loss of face among this legalistic Jewish contingent from Jerusalem and also withdrew. He who had preached to the Gentiles (Acts 13:42–43) now "was led astray by their [Peter's and the other Jews'] hypocrisy" (Gal. 2:13).

3. These sad examples of an all-too-common phenomenon show how the immediate pressure of earthly reputation within a narrow circle can make a person lose his theological mind for an instant. To curry immediate social acceptance, Peter and Barnabas forsook their knowledge of the glory and power of the new covenant. Their temporary doctrinal insanity seemed to consist of the attitude, "Avoid any conflict with the immediately prevailing drift of the political

winds." They succumbed to their pride in the flesh of Abraham and hid the transforming power of the faith of Abraham under a cloud of ceremonialism. In this instance, the ceremonial does not lead to a deeper grasp of the moral (as it certainly did prior to the completed work of Christ) but becomes its antagonist.

Sylvia's Comments (vv. 11–13)

Even mature apostles weren't perfect. Peter himself caved in to those who wanted the Gentiles to keep the law too. Not only did he act hypocritically but he also influenced the other Jews to do so. Paul saw what happened and included this to remind us of how easy it is to get off track. Fear of man took precedence over fear of God. A trusted leader can easily sway others, so it is important to walk hand-in-hand daily with the truth. Sometimes we give in little by little until, like the proverbial frog, we are boiled up and served for dinner.

B. Paul Rebukes Peter (v. 14)

This troubling bit of inconsistency gives Paul an opportunity to demonstrate his uncompromised grasp of the gospel in which there is "neither Jew nor Greek ... neither slave nor free ... no male and female" (Gal. 3:28). No distinction, whether of culture, politics, or creation, prohibits any divine image-bearer from finding the free pardon of sins in Jesus Christ. Christ has destroyed the middle wall of partition set up by ordinances (Eph. 2:11–15). If we are to be united with Christ in His single reconciling work on the cross, we must be united to one another by a deeper reality than merely typical ceremonies. As descendants of the first man in whose fall we all have sinned, we are united, for "there is no distinction" (Rom. 3:22). The solution to this fall under condemnation also is a point of absolute unity, for only one man in one single event has satisfied this susceptibility to condemnation (Rom. 3:28–31), pushed aside the ceremonial law of temporal division, and honored the law of eternal truth.

1. Peter's credentials as an apostle were formidable. As referenced above, he had been taught by a vision from heaven that he was not to call any person unclean. After this vision, he immediately went to a house filled with Gentiles and delivered a gospel message blessed with effectual power from the Holy Spirit, and he saw Gentiles converted (Acts 10:1–48). He referred to this event in defending the right of the Gentiles to gospel privileges without their embracing the ceremonial law (Acts 11:17–18). God had granted the Gentiles repentance unto life.

2. Now, however, Paul points out with painful honesty the destructive hypocrisy of Peter on this issue in this particular event. Note that he emphasized that their action amounted to this: "They were not straightforward about the truth of the gospel" (NKJV), or "their conduct was not in step with the truth of the gospel" (v. 14). "If you, though a Jew, live like a Gentile and not like a Jew, how can you force the Gentiles to live like Jews?" (v. 14). Paul was reminding Peter that Peter himself had been instrumental, through divine revelation, in breaking the Jew/Gentile barrier. He is

saying, "Since you have seen and practiced accordingly, Peter, that the ceremonies are null and void and you are free to go to a Gentile house and even 'to remain for some days' (Acts 10:48), why do you now act as if the Gentiles are not worthy to be in your presence unless they consent to the ceremonies which you have formerly destroyed?"

3. How could Paul make the point with any greater power that these Judaizers are setting forth a "different gospel" (Gal 1:6)? Likewise, how could he demonstrate with greater power his standing as an uncompromised apostle, faithful to the revealed truth of the gospel, than this public reprimand of Peter and Barnabas? His credentials to demand the obedient attention of the Galatian churches were flawless. That this did not destroy the relationship between Paul and Peter but actually led to a deeper endearment we find in the language of Peter in 2 Peter 3:15–16, where he wrote of his "beloved brother Paul," and placed his writings among the "Scriptures." If the gospel is loved first, then those who have unbounded clarity as to its contents and immovable love for its proclamation are among our most valued friends.

Sylvia's Comments (v. 14)

Paul steps up with the truth and confronts this revered, respected leader. He calls him out for behaving one way when he's not being watched by the false judges and another way when they are around. He speaks forcefully to Peter to get him to see his sin. From what we see in the rest of Scripture, we can be certain Peter returned to faithfully living for Christ.

III. A Precise, Authenticating, Biblical Argument (2:15–21)

It is possible that what follows is still part of Paul's response to Peter. On the other hand, it could be an independent analysis of the doctrinal implications of this event. To me, it seems that Paul gives a quick summary of his continued reasoning with Peter and expands it with his own theological discourse.

A. Using Peter's Own Words (v. 15)

Paul now takes his cue from some of the words of Peter himself. Obviously knowing of Peter's revelatory reconciliation to Gentile missions, Paul gave an intense, distilled exposition of the gospel of justification by faith. Peter had preached to the house of Cornelius, "To him all the prophets bear witness that everyone who believes in him receives forgiveness of sins through his name" (Acts 10:43). Later in his report at Jerusalem, Peter said, "If then God gave the same gift to them as he gave to us when we believed in the Lord Jesus Christ, who was I that I could stand in God's way?" (Acts 11:17).

Paul used that event by introducing his argument with the irony of the ceremonialist Jews' way of thinking: "We ourselves are Jews by birth [that is, born in the ethnic line of Abraham and the recipient of the mark of the covenant], and not Gentile sinners [sinners in their provenance from a non-covenanted people]" (v. 15).

It is the distinction between these two classes being adjudicated in the gospel. In essence, such concepts no longer are valid, for "all have sinned" and no person can see the kingdom of God without the new birth.

C. A Well-Constructed Chiasm (v. 16)

Note how Paul constructs the summary of Peter's statements into an intense and well-constructed chiasm that has the force of an irrefutable syllogism of universal application:

> ***a.*** A person is not justified by the works of the law.
>
> ***b.*** A person is justified by faith in Jesus Christ.
>
> ***c.*** This implies a conclusion of universal application of belief: "We also"—that is, the Jews—"have believed in Christ Jesus,"
>
> ***c'.*** implying that what is necessary for all the rest of mankind applies also in the same way to them—"have believed in Christ Jesus,"
>
> ***b'.*** so that we might be justified by faith in Christ Jesus
>
> ***a'.*** and not by works of the law.

This chiasm implies a universal application about the works of the law: "For by the works of the law no flesh will be justified."

D. A Changed Moral Status? *(vv. 17–19)*

Does the work of Christ, therefore, mean that those who formerly were "not sinners" have been made sinners by His work (v. 17)?

Is this moral irony actually the case, that Jews formerly were righteous and the children of God, and now, through the fulfillment of the messianic promises in Jesus of Nazareth, their moral status has been changed? Is the death of Christ a merely arbitrary way of making mortal the children of God so that some essential change has occurred in the status of the Jews because of Christ's obedience unto death? Is Christ, therefore, a minister of sin? Has His death constituted people as sinners who before were not sinners? Paul rejects the notion in no uncertain terms ("Certainly not!" [ESV]; "May it never be!" [NASB95]), for it is completely antithetical to the entire foundation of Christ's mission and contradicts the manner in which this mission must be accomplished. It is a conclusion that would involve an absolute misconstruing of the law.

1. If Peter, as well as Paul, received Christ by faith for the remission of sins in response to the convicting power of the law (Rom. 7:7–12, especially 13), and then they seek to reconstruct their former adherence to the law as the means of righteousness, they simply prove that they had not truly embraced the purpose of the law (v. 18). They had not concluded, given this hypothetical "rebuilding" of the law, with unimpeachable certainty, that they were unrighteous and needed both forgiveness for sin and the merit of another imputed to them for entrance into eternal

life. If that is indeed the case, they are yet in their sins. In doing this, Paul would prove himself "to be a transgressor" oblivious to the true and immutably holy standards of the law and unresponsive to its purpose to lead us to Christ.

2. But, in fact, "through the law," Paul affirmed, "I died to the law," that is, as the way of achieving righteousness (v. 19). From this death, life emerged. This death to the law as his path to saving righteousness brought him life before God, for it had the effect of seeing the true ministry of Christ for sinners. To this glorious redemptive transaction, he now turns.

Sylvia's Comments (vv. 15–19)

Paul contrasts origins between Jews and Gentiles: Jews were chosen to be God's people, set apart by the law; Gentiles were left to themselves without a pathway to God outside of the law. Here we get into the very heart of the gospel: people cannot be justified by works but only through faith in Christ. He repeats this in a different way. Jews must believe in Christ to be justified before God. Jews and Gentiles alike stand on equal footing with God through faith. Why does Paul call justification in Christ an endeavor? Maybe, as Jews, the accusation that they were sinners—that is, like the Gentiles—was repulsive. The law was designed to reveal sin and our need for a Savior. Christ is not the one who brings sin. Certainly not! He lived by the law to point us to our need for forgiveness, not to whip us into shape to once again keep the law. "Rebuilding the law" only shows our inability to keep the law. The law kills, so we must die to its demands and admit our need for Christ, the perfect law keeper, our Savior. Through Christ, we will always live to God.

E. A Substitionary and Propitiatory Death (v. 20)

Rather than trusting in any supposed righteousness he had based on the law (Phil. 3:9), Paul now sees the crucifixion of Christ as his own crucifixion, his own execution for his sins, consummated in another who took his place.

Christ's death was particularly substitutionary as well as fully propitiatory (wrath enduring) for the sake of all Christ's sheep.

Sylvia's Comments (vv. 20–21)

For his own part, a Jew of Jews, Paul relied only on faith in Christ, the Son of God, who took on human flesh and died an excruciating death through crucifixion. Through faith, we were crucified with Christ. We have been freed from the bondage of sin by the righteous Christ living in us. No longer do we live outside of faith but always united to Christ through faith, even while we are still in the flesh. Why? Because we are eternally loved and secured by God's grace. Nor can we add to Christ's sacrifice by keeping the law. Making the law a necessary part of salvation means that Christ's sacrifice was not enough to justify us—making it, in fact, useless.

---

1. Paul, having a secure knowledge of his election by the eternal covenantal grace of God (Gal. 1:15), sees his identity with Christ at the time of Christ's

crucifixion. "I have been crucified with Christ" (2:20). In eternity, Paul and all the elect were chosen in Christ (Eph. 1:4). So now, in time, their union with Him in death means they receive all His redemptive work secured (Rom. 8:32; Eph. 1:7).

2. Having been so crucified in the ransom paid by another, Paul can say in another place (1 Cor. 6:20) "for you were bought with a price," and conclude here that "it is no longer I who live" (Gal. 2:20) but rather, on account of Jesus's resurrection, demonstrating that death has been defeated, "Christ who lives in me." I do not, I must not, claim my life as my own if Christ has died for me, for I am ransomed and have been redeemed by His blood. The life I have now and the promise of life eternal have come only by that saving work of Christ.

3. "Though I still live in this dying world and in this dying flesh," Paul continued, "by the grace of God manifested in the death of Christ, I have been transferred to a new sphere." This present life is lived by "faith in the Son of God" (v. 20). The eternally generated, beloved Son of God has paid a price of infinite value. Now Paul affirms, "I trust in Him, I capitulate to Him and His righteousness and death all things that were supposed gains for me in this life." The identity of the Christian is in Christ. I must not find my most meaningful identity in any worldly category but only in Christ. In fact, we "are all one in Christ Jesus" (Gal. 3:28).

4. I have forsaken, so the theological testimony insisted, the arrogance implied in thinking that any conformity

to ceremonial law contributes to the salvation granted through Christ alone. Instead, I simply must confess and rely on this alone: He loved me in the eternal covenant of redemption and gave Himself up for me as He bore my sins in His own body on the tree.

> *I need no other argument,*
> *I need no other plea;*
> *It is enough that Jesus died,*
> *And that He died for me.*

F. Righteousness Not through the Law (v. 21)

The damning danger of clinging to the law as a means of right standing before God is that it eliminates our dependence on grace and therefore renders the redemptive obedience of Christ as a needless event. "If righteousness comes through the law, then Christ died for no purpose" (v. 21).

We are placed on our own if we seek to contribute any righteousness through any kind of personal obedience to the law (3:10). If we are on our own, we certainly will be found to be transgressors and still under condemnation. A bleeding and dying Christ completely destroys any construal of self-righteousness and makes all people of whatever provenance, ethnicity, gender, or social status come by way of the cross.

Chapter 4

The Law Kills—
The Spirit Gives Life

Galatians 3:1–14

I. Paul Issues a Series of Searching Questions (3:1–6)

A. Fooled by Enchantment (v. 1)

1. In his first question, "Who has bewitched you?" Paul challenges their clarity of thinking. He addresses them ("O foolish Galatians!") using a strong word meaning "mindless." This implies that such notions are without any rational grounds but could only have been smuggled in by some kind of enchantment. Certainly, they have not been convinced by a properly arranged exegetical and theological

argument. They simply have been hoodwinked by a mere manifestation of apparent, but unreal, authority. An idea has been conjured before them from the deep secrets of a skilled magician opposed to the pure righteousness of God.

Sylvia's Comments (v. 1)

After presenting his credentials and refocusing on Christ's crucifixion, Paul shakes his head and throws up his hands. As a friend of mine says, "What are you thinking?" Extremely emotional now, he points out what they saw with their own eyes, Christ crucified. What else do they need?

---

2. The position they received from his teaching was the straightforward, clear presentation of a historical work. Paul's preaching, written before them, as it were (the Greek word *proegraphe* means to have an argument written before one's eyes), called on them to consider, contemplate, weigh the arguments, and draw a rational conclusion as to what the crucifixion of Christ meant.

3. Paul's theology of the cross was given full display as he preached to them. When they believed his message, they believed that we cannot be right with God by human works of righteousness of any sort but only by the completed work of Christ.

B. A No-and-Yes Question (v. 2)

Paul's next question, "Did you receive the Spirit by works

of the law or by hearing with faith?" has two parts, the first part to be answered no, and the second, yes.

1. He asks them to recall how they received the gift of the Spirit. Was the Spirit given in response to their works of righteousness conforming to the whole law of God? Surely, they knew this was not the case. Both Jews and Gentiles had believed Paul's preaching, and it was clear that the works of the law had nothing to do with their being received by God as His children (Gal. 4:5–6) or being granted the gift of eternal life. When they believed, it was in response to the preaching of Paul and Barnabas (Acts 14:27). Their message would have set forth justification solely by Christ's righteousness made effectual in His death and resurrection and imputed to sinners solely by faith. The answer, therefore, clearly is "No, we did not receive the Spirit by works of the law."

2. Or was it in fact a belief in the message that Paul had preached? The answer is "Yes, we received the Spirit by the hearing of faith." Grammatically this could be paraphrased, "The kind of hearing that arises from faith."

   • Forgiveness, justification, the presence of the Spirit in giving hope, assurance, sanctification, and distribution of gifts all flow from what Christ, and Christ alone, has done. This is the message the Spirit blesses with true faith and His consequent sanctifying presence. "Did you receive this by faith or as a reward for your own performance of some work of the law?"

- When they believed Paul's message, the Gentiles had not been instructed in any of the details of the ceremonial law. Jews were present in the cities of Galatia, and they opposed the message of Paul, but the people of Galatia had believed despite the Jewish persecution of Paul (Acts 14:1–28). They believed Paul's message of sin, judgment, Christ's atonement, and resurrection. God had "opened a door of faith to the Gentiles" (Acts 14:27).

- In Romans 10, Paul discusses the unbelief of Israel in terms of the relation between hearing and believing: "How then will they call on him in whom they have not believed? . . . They have not all obeyed the gospel. . . . So then faith comes from hearing, and hearing through the word of Christ" (verses 14, 16–17). By the work of the Spirit, who opens the ears and shines in the heart, gospel truth carries with it its own evidence. Belief means to place absolute trust in the provision for sin as reported in the gospel message. Only the Spirit of God grants this kind of belief.

- Paul knew well that the operations of the Spirit of God in power had come with both external and internal manifestations, granting both salvation in true faith and showing power through miraculous works (Acts 14:1–3). None of this had come in response to their attempts at law-keeping but solely through the hearing of faith. "Yes, the hearing of faith."

3. Paul was well-acquainted with the religious appearance of this temptation to embrace a self-achieved

righteousness. He had been of that persuasion himself and saw clearly the zeal the Jews maintained for it. "For I bear them witness that they have a zeal for God, but not according to knowledge. For, being ignorant of the righteousness of God, and seeking to establish their own, they did not submit to God's righteousness. For Christ is the end of the law for righteousness to everyone who believes" (Rom. 10:2–4).

C. A Foolish Path (v. 3)

Paul's third question assumes right answers to both parts of the second question.

1. Again, Paul introduces the question with an indication of the empty-headedness of their developing inclination to legalism: "Are you so foolish?" He proceeds to challenge the consistency and clarity of their thinking: "Having begun by the Spirit, are you now being perfected by the flesh?"

2. Knowing how the gospel came to them, how they were taught by Paul even amid Jewish opposition, are they now going to fall into the trap of Jewish ceremonialism for the maturing of their faith? If true saving faith originated through the hearing of the gospel and by the work of the Spirit, do they now believe that by the power of the flesh they will be brought to spiritual maturity and make greater attainments toward true holiness by a series of observations of Jewish ceremonies?

3. Paul's introduction of the relation between Spirit and flesh anticipates his argument concerning the

relation of the Spirit's sanctifying operations in relation to the holiness of the law in 5:16–26.

D. Believing in Vain? (v. 4)

The fourth question points to the possible vanity of
their experience in Christ. "Did you suffer so many
things in vain?"

There are two ways in which one's belief could be in vain:

1. They could believe a message, the leading feature of
   which never actually occurred. This was the kind of
   vanity referred to in 1 Corinthians 15:2, 13–14. If
   Christ is not raised from the dead, then believing a
   message—the efficacy of which depends on the resurrection—is vain. If the resurrection did not occur,
   then believing it for eternal life is preposterous, and
   such a belief is empty.

2. On the other hand, the vanity of belief could be in
   the unsettled nature of the belief itself. Paul asked if
   the entirety of their previous experience of the gospel
   was an empty charade. In essence, he asks, "Did you
   feel the convicting power of the Spirit and see the
   demonstration of miraculous powers among you with
   no real internal change in your hearts and no firm
   conviction of the gospel's truth in your mind? Did
   you see and hear the gospel preached amid hateful
   opposition without grasping the eternal importance
   of it? Did you not think that the message we preached
   had the element of absoluteness about it? When we
   proclaimed that human efforts to achieve saving
   righteousness through any element of the law would
   always fall short, were vanity in themselves, and that

we could be justified only by what Christ Himself has done, that we were leaving something out? Did we rob you of the full truth amid our suffering?" He issues a similar warning to the Colossians when he reminds them they would be presented blameless and above reproach in the sight of God "if indeed you continue in the faith, stable and steadfast, not shifting from the hope of the gospel that you heard" (Col. 1:23).

3. This does not contradict the truth of the perseverance of the saints. Those whom God has foreknown—that is, loved graciously in the eternal covenant of redemption—will without fail be brought to the final state of glory (John 6:39–40; Rom. 8:29–30; Phil. 1:6). The query about suffering so many things in vain points to two realities:

- Some appear to believe and for a while attach themselves to a Christian community but in the end manifest that their type of "belief" was not saving faith. So it was with the believing Pharisees who turned out to be "false brothers." So it was with Simon Magus in Acts 8:12–13, 20–23.

- This shows the need for the consistent use of the means of grace—prayer, instruction, and worship—for the certifying and strengthening of the faith of God's elect and their knowledge of the truth that accords with godliness (Titus 1:1).

E. What Then? (v. 5)

Having energized their minds in thinking about theological truth, Paul returns to the first question issued in verse 2.

In verse 5, he wants their response by reissuing the question. Now, however, he has made them reason through the issue and begins the reiteration with a short but pithy phrase— *"ho oun"*—"What, then," "Therefore," or "So then," depending on one's translation. The phrase means, "Now that we have had this lesson in theology, let us look with reinformed eyes and hearts at the original question." Simply reiterated, Paul wants them to answer these queries: "Are all the blessings and riches of life in Christ and the presence of the Holy Spirit given as a result of works of the law or a response of sincere and full trust in the gospel? Are God's gifts rewards to you amid your imperfection or are they rewards granted for the sake of Christ and the provisions resident in His perfect obedience?" Having prompted the doctrinal exercise, he expects a fully convinced response consistent with the gospel that he preached to them.

F. Paul Points to Abraham (v. 6)

Paul caps off his questions by pointing to Abraham. According to the false teachers, Abraham was clearly the paradigm for the maintenance of circumcision. Paul takes their strongest argument and completely refocuses the alignment. Abraham is not a testimony to the perpetuity of circumcision but one for the central importance of faith.

Sylvia's Comments (vv. 2–6)

Paul asks them how they came to believe and then points out the answer: by the Spirit. Again, he calls them foolish for even thinking about going back to the law and working to perfect themselves—a foolish, impossible task. To believe such a thing is incomprehensible to Paul. He saw how they suffered for believing in Christ and reminds them. He reminds them of the miracles God has done because of faith, not by works of the law. He even refers to the father of the Jews, Abraham, who believed God and was declared righteous. His works were not what made him righteous; God declared him to be righteous because of his faith in God's faithfulness to His promises.

II. Intensifying the Argument Concerning Abraham (3:7–9)

Paul continues his discussion of Abraham to cement the answer to his questions in their consciences. Faith and imputation form the core substance, not circumcision.

A. By Faith Alone

The lasting universal significance of Abraham is not circumcision but faith.

1. According to Genesis 15:6, Abraham "believed the Lord, and he counted it to him as righteousness." Circumcision was not given as a covenantal sign until Genesis 17. Faith and righteousness preceded the giving of the sign of circumcision (Gen. 17:10–11).

2. The concept of imputation drives the relation of God to Abraham.

   - The word *counted* (also *imputed, reckoned*) indicates the certainty and accuracy of a mathematical formula or the conclusion of a well-constructed syllogism. The contents of Abraham's faith matched exactly the requirements indicated in the divine promise.

- In citing this Scripture in Romans 4:22, Paul explains, "No unbelief made him waver concerning the promise of God, but he grew strong in his faith as he gave glory to God, fully convinced that God was able to do what he had promised" (Rom. 4:20–21). That God Himself would perform all that was necessary for the fulfillment of the promise constituted the substance of righteousness—not a righteousness of Abraham but a righteousness of God imputed to Abraham.

- In Romans 4:8, the same term is used for the non-imputation of sin in the citation from Psalm 32. By that, Paul affirms that the idea of imputation precisely meets the just demands of God's law. For God not to reckon the results of our sins to belong to us means He has found a way to be "just and also the justifier" (Rom. 3:26). The perfect answer to our absolute debt to the law has been given so that its penalty has been fully enacted and truthfully computed as paid.

B. A Promise of Blessings

Paul draws this conclusion from the clear implications of the promise given to Abraham before he was given the mark of circumcision.

In Genesis 12:1–3, God promised Abraham two things: "I will make of you a great nation" and "In you all the families of the earth shall be blessed." The first of these promises concerned his physical lineage, and the second referred to the universal implications of the continuity of this physical lineage. Circumcision would be the mark by which Abraham's physical lineage would be traced, but the blessings to all the nations would be the fruit of faith verified and sealed through the means of sacrifice (Gen. 15:6–21).

C. An Airtight Conclusion

Those who seek, therefore, to make circumcision—or any aspect of obedience to the law, either ceremonial or moral—the cause of salvation misunderstand the significance of Abraham and the place of circumcision in his relationship with God.

Paul's demonstration of this aspect of biblical theology is amazingly brief but airtight in its conclusion.

Sylvia's Comments (vv. 7–9)

The false teachers are probably hearing these words, and the reference to Abraham catches their ears. Paul expands his point: (1) The sons of Abraham are the sons of faith, not the law; (2) God would justify the Gentiles by faith; (3) God told Abraham all nations would receive God's blessing; therefore, (4) all who have faith in God are blessed, just as Abraham was blessed, because of faith.

III. An Argument from the Intended Operation of the Law (3:10–14)

The irony, as well as the deadly error, of the Judaizers'

triumphalistic invasion of the churches consists of a complete misreading of the law. They taught that it brought acceptance, not a curse. They made a purely symbolic ceremony into pure moral uprightness. Their attempts to achieve a right standing destroyed the exclusive source of righteousness.

A. A Universal Curse (v. 10)

The present effect of the law is a universal curse on all lawbreakers. Paul points to the statement of curses issued from Mount Ebal in Deuteronomy 27 that ends with this specific curse: "Cursed be anyone who does not confirm the words of this law by doing them" (v. 26). Paul knew the foundation of the law was aimed at the heart and that, because the human heart is corrupt, none has ever kept the law in its true spiritual intent (Rom. 7:9–13). All humanity fallen in Adam live consistently and universally under the curse and cannot extricate themselves from it for they can never become perfect law-keepers.

B. Resting on Faith (v. 11)

That explains why justification is presented as resting on faith. Paul looks not only to Abraham but to God's Word as given to Habakkuk during a time of impending judgment on Israel, when this fulsome phrase was stated, "Behold the proud, his soul is not upright in him; but the just shall live by his faith" (Hab. 2:4 NKJV). There is the way of pride, which has to do with the confidence one places in his own righteousness; conversely, there is the way of faith, which has to do with full trust in the goodness, righteousness, prerogative, mercy, and holy purpose of God. Faith involves a mistrust of self and full belief in God's words and works. Faith abandons hope in one's personal moral or ceremonially religious standing and rests all in the person and work of Jesus of Nazareth, the righteous Redeemer. By faith alone, a sinner finds life.

C. The Law Is Not of Faith (v. 12)

The law blesses only those who keep it without any failure and is the antithesis of salvation by faith.

1. Surely it is true that the perfect righteousness of the law would convey life, even eternal life according to the covenant of works established by God with Adam in the garden of Eden.

2. The law, therefore, is not of faith, for its way of giving life is through unshadowed perfection in actions and in heart. The law does not allow for trust in the accomplishment of another but requires all from the one subject to its authority. The law demands an unfailing practice of all that is involved in perfect, uncompromised, submissive love as the perpetual motive from which flows every righteous act.

3. Of Christ alone was this true, as prophesied in Psalm 22:9–10, "You are he who took me from the womb; you made me trust you at my mother's breasts. On you was I cast from my birth, and from my mother's womb you have been my God." The "trust" the psalmist mentioned means a sense of submission and dependence on the divine will, fitting for the understanding that a creature has toward the Creator. It is

not the trust in the righteousness of another but a full and loving submission to God's will.

4. Never, from the moment of conception until He consummated His obedience in the bloody death on the cross, dying as a propitiation for our sins, did Jesus do anything but find delight in the pursuit of submission to His Father's will. It is not our obedience, therefore, by which we find life. Christ Himself is our life. "For you have died, and your life is hidden with Christ in God. When Christ who is your life appears, then you also will appear with him in glory" (Col. 3:3–4).

D. A Perfect Synthesis (vv. 13–14)

Only in Christ do we find a perfect synthesis of the operations of the law and the promise to Abraham.

1. As moral agents made in the image of God, the covenant of works still is in authority over us, and having violated it, we are under a curse. For its fulfillment, one must die. By His own blood, Christ has purchased us and redeemed us from the sentence of death by taking our place under the curse. As an infinitely glorious person fully capable of representing creatures, He removed the curse.

2. The promise that Abraham would be a blessing to all nations and that "all the ends of the world shall remember and turn to the LORD, and all the families of the nations shall worship before you" (Ps. 22:27) found its moral basis in the grace of the suffering servant, Christ Jesus. Even as Abraham was counted

righteous by faith, so "it shall be told of the LORD to the coming generation; they will come and proclaim his righteousness to a people yet unborn, that he has done it" (Ps. 22:30–31).

3. The "promised Spirit" (ESV) or "promise of the Spirit" (v. 14 NKJV) means that the promise given to Abraham becomes the possession of all his spiritual posterity in the effectual operation, indwelling presence, sustaining power, and spiritual circumcision of the heart performed by the Spirit as the mark of the new covenant people of God: "For in Christ Jesus you are all sons of God, through faith" (3:26); "For through the Spirit, by faith, we ourselves eagerly wait for the hope of righteousness. For in Christ Jesus neither circumcision nor uncircumcision counts for anything, but only faith working through love" (5:5–6).

4. The Second London Baptist Confession summarizes many of the ideas in this text in its first paragraph on "Justification" in chapter XI:

> Those God effectually calls He also freely justifies. He does this, not by infusing righteousness into them but by pardoning their sins and accounting and accepting them as righteous. He does this for Christ's sake alone and not for anything produced in them or done by them. He does not impute faith itself, the act of believing, or any other gospel obedience to them as their righteousness. Instead, He imputes Christ's active obedience to the whole law and passive

obedience in His death as their whole and only righteousness by faith. This faith is not self-generated; it is the gift of God.

Sylvia's Comments (vv. 10–14)

Paul now picks up with the law and what Scripture says about people who rely on it. Wow! Those people are under a curse because it is impossible for fallen man to do every jot and tittle of the law. Even Adam and Eve could not keep the law, and they were not yet fallen. Paul continues to contrast works of the law and the gift of faith:

- The law doesn't make anyone righteous; faith does.
- The law cannot take the place of faith because it is futile striving.
- Christ came under the curse of the law in our place; the righteous One was killed in the place of the unrighteous.

Why? So all the nations could have blessings and life by the Spirit because of faith, not works.

Chapter 5

God Provided a Mediator

Galatians 3:15–4:7

I. The Unchanging Promise of God to Abraham (3:15–18)

The promise to Abraham was given prior to any other arrangements and is thus the sole basis of divine favor. The unchangeableness of a will, or covenantal arrangement, is recognized even in human society.

A. Humans Take Wills Seriously (v. 15)

Paul gives "a human example" in verse 15 to explain his point. When a will is finally ratified, no conditions can be added. The legal standing of the will takes precedence over personal objections or additions by which other parties may seek to amend without the approval of the parties originally interested in the contract.

B. To Whom Was the Promise Made? (v. 16)

Even so, God has made a promise to Abraham and to his "offspring."

1. Paul points out (v. 16) that the word *offspring* is singular, and—though it includes the sons of Israel in the physical promise and all believers in the spiritual blessings (see v. 29)—the ultimate fulfillment of this promise is found only in Jesus Christ. It is in Him that all the promises are "Yes" and "Amen" (2 Cor. 1:20). The promise given to Abraham was given to Christ before time began (Titus 1:2).

2. The faith by which righteousness comes is in Christ alone. The removal of the universal curse of sin is in Christ alone. The blessing to the nations, therefore, comes in Christ alone. The offspring to whom all the promises refer is summed up in Christ.

Sylvia's Comments (vv. 15–16)

When we sign a covenant or contract, we must have witnesses and possibly a notary to verify it. It is then delivered to the right authorities to file as law. It is an official record and cannot be altered. This is what happened when God told Abraham that faith yields righteousness. God promised this as ongoing and unchangeable.

C. No New Requirements (v. 17)

When the law was given, therefore, 430 years after the promise was made to Abraham, it did not introduce a new set of requirements that placed a condition on the certainty of the promise.

An unconditional promise arises from reasons in the mind and purpose of the "promiser," not from any subsequent set of circumstances that might accrue to the one to whom the promise was made.

D. An Inheritance through a Promise (v. 18)

God made an unconditional promise to Abraham, a thing He could do, for the purpose already was sealed in eternity.

Though this promise brought about a series of relationships and other covenants that included conditions, none of those rendered the original covenant with Abraham unworkable. They simply indicated all the conditions that would be fulfilled by the final "offspring" through whom the promise to Abraham would be perfectly fulfilled.

Sylvia's Comments (vv. 17–18)

When God gave the law to Moses and the Israelites as they traveled from Egypt to the land He promised, He did not discard what He declared previously to Abraham and his offspring. God's promise stands!

II. The Law Locked Sinners In; Faith Sets Them Free (3:19–29)

What is the relation of law to promise? If God's promise to Abraham was unconditional, why did He impose the law upon the physical descendants of Abraham? If the moral law is absolute, how does faith operate both to set us free as well as honor an unchangeable and curse-bringing standard of righteousness?

A. The Reality of Transgression (vv. 19–20)

1. That which made the promise necessary was the presence of sin. To make clear the aspects of the moral law written on the heart against which all mankind had rebelled and against which all were consistently transgressing, the law was given to Israel, the elect nation through whom the Messiah would come. The terms on which the promise would be fulfilled were set forth clearly in the law but would not affect the freeness of the promise to Abraham.

2. How was this given by angels? Angels are ministering spirits sent forth to minister for those who will inherit salvation (Heb. 1:14). Our text in Galatians 3:19 reveals they had a part in communicating the law to Moses.

3. Who is the mediator through whose agency this came?

   • It seems Moses was the mediator. He received the law and brought it down to the people (Exodus 20). He gave a detailed review and reassertion of it in the book of Deuteronomy (Deuteronomy 5).

- Christ is the prophet like Moses who also brings the law to us (Deut. 18:15). Unlike Moses, He not only brings the law to us but is the revealer of that law and, in His incarnation, the embodiment of its perfect fulfillment. Jesus is the righteousness the law requires.

4. The law stood as a constant reminder of the righteousness intrinsic to being creatures made in the image of God. It reminded the Israelites this universal expectation of righteousness was given by specific delineation only to them as the nation through whom that righteousness would finally be perfectly fulfilled. And how and when would that occur? "Until the offspring should come to whom the promise had been made" (v. 19). When the Offspring, the Seed (NKJV), would come and do His work, He would gain all the benefits of the promise and give them to the people given Him by the Father. Those, then, would be made "the righteousness of God in Him" (2 Cor. 5:21 NKJV).

5. Why is the singularity of God mentioned? Since God is one, and knowledge of the law comes through a mediator, then the fulfillment of the law also will come through a mediator. God is one party, and the other party must be represented by a mediator. If the communication of the law itself came through a mediator in light of the overpowering holiness of God (Exodus 19, see especially verses 18–22), how much more will the fulfillment of the law for a sinful people need a mediator (1 Tim. 2:5–6)?

Sylvia's Comments (vv. 19–20)

God, in His graciousness, gave the law to this particular race of people because they were sinners. How the scribes and Pharisees had twisted this! They thought because they had the law, they were righteous. But they had the law because they were sinners. God put it in place to give them guidance until the Offspring, Christ, came. God mediated for them, to them, and because of their need.

B. No Contrarianism (vv. 21–29)

Next, Paul argues that the law is not contrary to the promises of God.

1. There never was a time when the law was not operative (Rom. 5:13–14), and the first promise of life came in the context of perpetual obedience to a command. Disobedience would bring on immediate death; perpetual obedience would, therefore, avoid death in all its forms and imply the eventual confirmation in eternal life (Gen. 2:16–17).

2. Through righteousness, life is imparted. As with Adam, perfect righteousness merits eternal life. Now that transgression is a reality, no law can be given that will reverse the presence of transgression, and thus the law was not given to impart life. If a law had power to alter a person's moral disposition and status as well, God would not have put Himself to the expense of giving His Son to gain life.

3. Throughout Scripture, however, we learn that everyone is imprisoned under sin (v. 22).

- The historical narrative from Genesis 3 through Revelation 22 shows that we are unrighteous and filthy. Before the flood, "the wickedness of man was great in the earth," and "every intention of the thoughts of his heart was only evil continually" (Gen. 6:5). After the flood, when Noah built an altar before the Lord, and his family was the only family alive, the Lord said, "I will never again curse the ground because of man, for the intention of man's heart is evil from his youth." (Gen. 8:21). "He who is unjust, let him be unjust still; he who is filthy, let him be filthy still" (Rev. 22:11 NKJV).

- The propositions of Scripture testify in no uncertain terms and in many turns of phrase that "all have sinned and fall short of the glory of God" (Rom. 3:23), that "none is righteous, no, not one" (Rom. 3:10), and that "people loved darkness rather than the light because their works were evil" (John 3:19). Indeed, "the whole world lies in the power of the evil one" (1 John 5:19).

- If all are sinners, as the law confirms, then the moral guilt of sin must be cared for in the same way in every person. That way, graciously given by God in accordance with the original promise to Abraham, is by faith in Jesus Christ. All who believe, irrespective of their relation to the ceremonial law and even in light of their consistent course of disobedience to the moral law, find the promise fulfilled in Christ.

Sylvia's Comments (vv. 21–22)

God is about setting us free from sin and giving us life without death. The law could not do that. The law became the guard that should have constantly reminded the people they were condemned sinners apart from faith. Paul is reminding the Galatians that salvation through Christ by faith is what all the Scriptures teach.

4. The law served, therefore, as a guardian and a schoolmaster (vv. 23–24)—as the one, to show our guilt and need of intervention, and as the other, to point us to the one who could rescue us.

- "Before faith came" (v. 23) does not mean that faith had no reality prior to Christ. That would contradict Paul's point of Abraham's righteousness being by faith. Faith is used in a substantive sense, meaning the person and the events that would constitute the body of truths to be believed. The one in whom faith is to be placed came when Jesus came.

- "We were held captive" (v. 23). As a guardian, the law would not let us out of captivity to its demands for perfect righteousness and established the fact that its demands would only be met by faith.

- On that basis, the law taught us to expect this deliverance from guilt and the meeting of the demands in the person of another—the Christ sent by God. The guardian did not let us gain confidence in another. The schoolmaster allowed us to find hope in Christ alone, "our tutor to bring us to Christ, that we might be justified by faith" (v. 24). So, the tutor said, "In righteousness you shall be established; you shall be far from oppression, for you shall not fear" (Isa. 54:14).

5. Our being under a guardian and tutor has now given way to sonship (verses 25–26). Faith in Christ shows that the law's task has been done. The law does not linger to claim a part in justification but turns us over to Christ in whom alone we find justification, and not only so, but reception into the family of God to become heirs.

- "For as many of you as were baptized into Christ have put on Christ" (v. 27). The phrase "baptized into Christ" is also used in Romans 6:3. There the baptism is "into His death," meaning by baptism we symbolize our union with the benefits of Christ's obedience. Jesus Himself entered into baptism under John for He had another baptism with which to be baptized, that is, His death. The "faith in Christ Jesus" of verse 26 (NKJV) has preceded the "baptized into Christ" of verse 27. Being clothed with Christ, therefore, means that by faith we partake of the benefits of Christ's own baptism unto death in which He took away the sins of all who would unite with Him by faith. The ordinance of baptism testifies that even as the water covers the entire body, so by faith have you been covered with Christ and His perfect obedience. Not one whit of our person remains exposed to wrath, for, like baptism fully engulfs us, so Christ's righteousness clothes us, leaving no place for God's wrath to rest. Baptism is the visible picture of our lives being hid with Christ in God (Col. 3:3).

- Now, differences of religious background, social status, or gender constitute no barrier to the freeness of salvation in Christ (v. 28). A guilty man may be justified by the same blood and righteousness as a guilty woman. A Jew may be justified, and indeed, must be justified, by the same blood and righteousness as a guilty Greek. A guilty slave may, and must, be justified by the same blood and righteousness as a guilty freeman. The temporal status is not eliminated in this life, but neither does it hinder perfect unity and equality in Christ.

- To belong to Christ is to belong to the sphere in which the promise to Abraham is fulfilled (v. 29). Jesus Christ, being the true "seed" of Abraham as well as the "seed" of the women promised in Genesis 3:15, grants sinners the status of "seed" or "offspring" through union with him by faith in his saving work.

Sylvia's Comments (vv. 23–29)

Paul keeps his language hardline. He doesn't soften the blow as he reiterates their foolishness. The law holds us captive, imprisoned, under guard. Faith in Christ frees, justifies, adopts, declares us sons of God and offspring, and makes us heirs. Not only these magnificent things, but our baptism shows that we have put on Christ and are one with Him and with other believers. No more are there Jew or

Greek, slave or free, male or female. No matter the color of our skin or national heritage, or political, social or economic standing, Christ makes us one with Him and each other. By faith, we are made righteous, free of sin, and forever pleasing to God.

III. An Eternal Inheritance in Due Time (4:1–7)

Paul uses an analogy of an heir under guardians until the child comes of age to embrace the inheritance as a son.

A. A Son as a Slave (vv. 1–3)

Paul shows how the elect are under the same condition in their natural state as everyone else.

1. Paul uses the earthly example that the heir of a massive estate does not receive it while he is a child. He has no more authority over the estate than does a slave of the same household.

2. Even so, those on whom God had placed His favor to bring to sonship, "predestined . . . for adoption to himself as sons through Jesus Christ" (Eph. 1:5), labor under the preparatory phase, the rudimentary principles, of God's plan until Christ comes. On a large scale, this reality constitutes the division of history into BC and AD. The people of God no longer are identified by ceremonial laws and rituals but by faith in Christ and evidence of a heart changed by the Holy Spirit. Likewise, every individual has the same division in his or her history—BC and AD.

Sylvia's Comments (vv. 1–3)

Paul compares our inheritance in Christ with the laws governing earthly inheritance. Until we have met the governing criteria, we cannot fully enjoy our inheritance, even though it is ours. Before faith in Christ, we were governed by the law. At a set time, established by God, those regulations and statutes were set aside to have no present or future hold on us.

B. The Perfect Time for Sonship (vv. 4–7)

Paul shows how the incarnation of Christ, the "fullness of time," broke the bonds of the time of anticipation. Paul goes deeper into his argument as to why the incarnation was necessary "to redeem those who were under the law" (4:5).

Sylvia's Comments (vv. 4–7)

We have been given insight into God's nature through creation, the fall, Noah, the prophets, and the kings. He revealed Himself in history, poetry, song, art, the tabernacle, the temple, and more. And then, at just the right time and place, He sent His Son. This Son, who now had a beating human heart pumping blood through veins, and lungs to take in air and cry for the food He needed to survive, was born to a woman who still lived under the law. But this birth of the One who would fulfill the law divided history. On the earth was now One who could fulfill the law and restore our relationship with God. The law kept us separate from God, but

we are now adopted into God's family as His children. Now we have the Spirit living in us. We are
no longer slaves, day by day working to keep each
aspect of the law and offer the right sacrifices to
justify us. The perfect sacrifice was made so that by
faith we are justified, set free from works, adopted
by God, and given an imperishable inheritance.

1. Now we see what type of redeemer is necessary. I
   say "necessary," for Paul has been arguing from the
   standpoint of necessity. In Galatians 2:21 Paul wrote,
   "I do not nullify the grace of God, for if righteousness were through the law, then Christ died for no
   purpose." Again in 3:21, "Is the law then contrary
   to the promises of God? Certainly not! For if a law
   had been given that could give life, then righteousness would indeed be by the law." In the context of
   redemption, Christ did not die needlessly; He died,
   therefore, of necessity—that is, Christ did not die
   without the need of it but precisely in view of the
   need of it. Since a law could not be given that would
   give life, the impartation of life must, of necessity,
   come through a means that fulfilled the law but tran-
   scended its "ability," therefore, necessarily.

2. This necessity is not an absolute necessity, for God
   could have justly willed not to redeem. Toward us,
   grace is pure gift. It does not arise from our worthiness
   but to show a facet of the glory of God that could not
   be seen apart from this work of salvation. The death
   of Christ, therefore, is a consequent necessity indis-
   pensable to God's will to redeem. Our being *under the*

82 | A Commentary on Galatians

law in the sense of under its condemnation made this kind of redemption necessary. How do redeemer and redemption unite as one and the same in this mysterious grace of God? Personal moral agents culpable to wrath because of corruption and transgression can be accepted to sonship only by the worthiness of a moral agent who is fit to be their substitute.

3. Unless he were a particular kind of person, even the death of an innocent man could not serve to atone for sins. So, "God sent forth his Son, born of woman" (4:4).

   • This work of the incarnation was an element of the eternal covenant of redemption in which the Father's part was to send His Son. This demonstrated the great love the Father had for those among His creatures whom He had elected to be His children (see Rom. 5:8; 1 John 4:9–10; Gal. 1:4).

   • The Son is the eternal Son of the Father, coequal in essence, co-creator, co-sustainer of the world and eternally the One who is the personal expression of God's nature and redemptive love (Heb. 1:2–4).

   • The Son's part in the covenant was to come in our nature so He could work in our stead. To do this, He had to be "born of a woman." This miracle of incarnation is described in Luke 1:35, in which we see the work of the Holy Spirit ("the Holy Spirit will come upon you"), the operation of the Father ("and the power of the Most High will overshadow you"), and the miraculous location of the Son in Mary's womb even though she was a virgin. "You will conceive in your womb and bear a son" (Luke 1:31).

- Jesus entered into human life the way all humans do. He was not a separately created humanity but one with us. The language surrounding the conception and birth narratives shows the reality of conception and normal human gestation: "Blessed is the fruit of your womb!"; "Mary . . . was with child"; "The time came for her to give birth. And she gave birth to her firstborn son" (Luke 1:42; 2:5–7).

- Without the instrumentality of a male and through the creative work of the Spirit, Mary's egg was fertilized and was assumed without division of time into the eternal person of the eternally generated Son of God. The prophecy to the serpent that his head would be crushed by her seed came to fruition (Gen. 3:15).

- The reality of His humanity is another of those things necessary for redemption. There was only one humanity to whom the law was given. There is only one humanity that fell and now stands in need of redemption. There is only one sphere, this present fallen world, within which this righteousness can be established. His true humanity, therefore, was necessary for the component parts of His justifying work.

  o His humanity was necessary for substitution (2 Cor. 5:21).

- o His humanity was necessary for righteousness (Rom. 5:19).

- o His humanity was necessary for resurrection (1 Cor. 15:21).

- o His humanity was necessary for His work as the Mediator (1 Tim. 2:5–6).

- o His humanity was necessary for His continued intercession (1 John 1:7 and 2:1–2).

- He was "born under the law" (v. 4). As a human like us, Jesus had all the demands of the law on Him personally. As our substitute, He also had to shoulder its curse for us to be forgiven. He obeyed all its righteous demands in establishing an unblemished righteousness by which we are justified; He died under its curse (Gal. 3:13), by which we are forgiven.

4. This work completed redemption from the demands of the law. Because He was "under the law," its demands have been satisfied by Him for those "who were under the law" (v. 5).

- All its ceremonial aspects (circumcision, sacrifices, priestly arrangements) have been fulfilled by Him and those parts of the law no longer place their burden on us, and thus, they are without any further need of execution. The types and prophecies contained in the ceremonies now stand fulfilled (Luke 2:21–22, 39; Heb. 10:1, 12).

- Since the law has but a shadow of the good things to come instead of the true form of these realities,

it can never, by the same sacrifices that are continually offered every year, make perfect those who
draw near. . . . But when Christ had offered for
all time a single sacrifice for sins, he sat down at
the right hand of God, waiting from that time
until his enemies should be made a footstool for
his feet. For by a single offering he has perfected
for all time those who are being sanctified. (Heb.
10:1, 12–14)

- Civil aspects of the law that defined Israel as a holy
nation are transformed in the work of Christ to
create a new people. They are not marked by the
development of external codes or festivals or use
of the sword for the enforcement of the civil code.
The forming of the holy nation, the Israel of God
(Gal. 6:16), comes by the drawing of people from
all nations and tribes and tongues for the distinc-
tive display of holiness (2 Cor. 6:16–7:1). The
moral law is embraced, not as a means of justification for us but as the substance of a fully sanctified
formation of Christ in us. This is now pursued not
in the strength of the flesh but through the regenerative work of the Spirit, expounded in 5:16–18.

- The law as a covenant of works for the purpose
of eternal life has been fulfilled by Him, so that
"whoever has the Son has life; whoever does not
have the Son of God does not have life" (1 John
5:12) but "the wrath of God remains on him"
(John 3:36). This mainly involved the fulfillment
of the moral law but includes a positive requirement, as it did with Adam.

o According to Romans 7:10, the law "that promised life" was at the same time an occasion for sin. As in Adam, so in us, the command brought death. This radical result of disobedience to the law shows that the "law is holy, and the commandment is holy and righteous and good" (Rom. 7:12). Galatians 3:12 affirmed the life-giving intent of the law: "The one who does them shall live by them."

o Romans 2:13 reiterates this original purpose: "for it is not the hearers of the law who are righteous in the sight of God, but the doers of the law who will be justified." Christ is the only doer of the law and therefore the only source of righteousness for our race.

o The positive requirement was tied to the moral character of the law. Jesus, as a perfectly righteous keeper of the law, did not have to die under its curse. But this commandment He received from His Father, that He would give His life in order to take it up again (John 10:18). He died, "the righteous for the unrighteous" (1 Peter 3:18), obeying a positive commandment (the kind of commandment Adam failed to keep). The only One who died under the law, not as a just punishment but as a substitutionary sacrifice, "redeemed us from the curse of the law by becoming a curse for us" (Gal. 3:13).

• The law, in its power of condemnation, therefore, has been removed in Christ by His work and in Christ only: "There is therefore now no condemnation for those who are in Christ Jesus" (Rom. 8:1).

5. In redemption, we also receive the adoption as sons.

- As a matter of Christ's unity of person in the incarnation, our humanity in Him has achieved the status of *Son of God* by the perfect course of His obedience. His humanity has consummated the perfect conformity to the divine law that was the goal of Adam's obedience in the garden of Eden. Perfect righteousness for justification and perfectly immutable holiness for sanctification were accomplished in the same course of obedience by Jesus, son of Mary. Now by our union with Him, not only are we justified by His righteousness, we are also sons of God in holiness.

- Even as Christ as the Son of God in His incarnation received the Spirit without measure (John 3:34–35), so now that we are adopted as Sons by redemptive union with Christ, God sends His Spirit into our hearts bearing witness of God as our Father (Gal. 4:6).

- As He has shared our humanity for redeeming us through His blood, so He gives us His Spirit that we might share His sonship. The Spirit vindicated him in His sonship (1 Tim. 3:16) and now witnesses to our sonship by His sanctifying presence.

- "So you are no longer a slave, but a son, and if a son, then an heir through God" (Gal. 4:7). Now being sons, all the riches of heaven, the presence of God, and the enjoyment of His glory constitute our inheritance. According to 1 Peter 1:3–4, this inheritance is one that is "imperishable, undefiled, and unfading, kept in heaven for you." This sonship is ours now by union with Christ and is being accomplished in our own spiritual and moral consciousness presently (Eph. 4:22–24) but will be consummated in true righteousness and holiness when Christ returns, and we shall be like Him (1 John 3:2–3).

Chapter 6

Son of Promise

Galatians 4:8–31

Paul continues his demonstration from Scripture that all people who are justified are "justified by faith in Christ and not by works of the law" (Gal. 2:16). That these Gentiles have been led out of paganism but are now flirting with the bondage of Jewish law astounds Paul. He seeks to show them from the law itself that the entire Old Testament revelation pointed to Christ as the only fulfillment of the law's righteous demands.

I. Ceremonial Judaism and Its Likeness to Paganism (4:8–11)

A. Oppressive Idolatry (v. 8)

When Paul came to the Galatians, they were entrenched in oppressive idolatry. Acts 14:8–18 records how zealous they were for pagan deities. Paul and Barnabas were barely able to restrain the people from offering sacrifices to them as gods.

B. God Acted (v. 9)

Their initial manifestation was evidence that God had acted toward them in grace apart from any work of theirs. Paul is careful in presenting the knowledge of God in its true light. It is true that we come to know God when we receive His revelation of truth, justice, and mercy as demonstrated in the cross of Christ. Such knowledge, however, is subsequent to God's initiation of salvation founded on His previous and eternal knowledge of us. Romans 8:29 says, "For those whom he foreknew he also predestined to be conformed to the image of his Son."

C. A Return to the Law? (v. 9)

Having started by grace and been rescued from a works-oriented, highly articulated pagan ceremonialism, do they now return to a works-oriented ceremonialism of Jewish hue?

In paganism, they sought the pleasure of the gods through following ceremonies and offering special sacrifices, as if they could please the deities and commend themselves to their favor by following specified regulations, rules, and rituals. How is that different from adopting a new set of regulations, rules, and rituals that no longer have their original intent and have been made obsolete by having been fulfilled in Christ? If they do this, they make themselves slaves again—bound to make themselves pleasing to God by self-righteousness rather than receiving righteousness as a gift.

D. Observing Rituals Again (v. 10)

They seem to have given themselves over to that which they escaped. As pagans, they had certain religious "days and months and seasons and years" and now are adopting a different set of the same religious rhythms. There is an essential difference between the biblical gospel of grace and all other religions based on works and rituals.

E. A Labor Worth Nothing? (v. 11)

Again, Paul brings up the possibility of vanity in his gospel labors toward them. He has suggested that original reception of the truth of salvation by Christ's sacrifice by faith generated and sealed by the Spirit of God might be vain. If, indeed, their initial suffering for such faith was vain (3:4), then his labor over them also was vain.

Sylvia's Comments (4:8–11)

When Paul says they did not know God, he's referring to life before faith. Under the law they were ignorant slaves with no understanding of the truth. Now, through faith in the justifying work of Christ, they have freedom and relationship with God. Paul is showing them they are going backward to the old ways of living. Paul's stridently making his point, calling their celebrations and rituals worthless and base. They are trading freedom for slavery and treasure for trash. At this point, he sees them rejecting the truth for lies. It looks like they've thrown out like a bucket of dirty water all he had poured into them.

II. A Gospel of High Value (4:12–16)

The value the Galatians placed on Paul's gospel message outstripped his physical weakness.

A. Ceased Resistance to Uncircumcised Gentiles (v. 12)

1. As Paul does in other places, he points to his own example as imitable in gospel issues. He sets forth imitation of him as a general principle in 1 Corinthians 4:14–16. As a specific example to the Thessalonians, he pointed to his tribulations as evidence that reception of the gospel would bring tribulation (1 Thess. 1:6). His labor among them was a demonstration that living by gospel truth meant personal responsibility for upkeep by labor (2 Thess. 3:7–9). His energetic pursuit of heavenly-mindedness was to be a model of the impact of gospel truth on desires for holiness (Phil. 3:14–17; 4:9). Now, his personal attitude toward the uncircumcised was to be followed as a substantial and necessary position on the fulfillment of ceremonial law.

2. Paul had forsaken a lifestyle dominated by Jewish ceremonial law and adopted a manner of social friendship, eating, and religious observation that ignored those former regulations in order to not shut himself off from the Gentiles, except in the area of moral observation of the law (Gal. 5:13–14; 1 Peter 1:1–5). In chapter 1, he referred to his "former life in Judaism" (v. 13), so rigorously antagonistic to the freedom of the gospel that he persecuted those who were Christians.

3. He asks them to follow him in this view of finding freedom from Jewish ceremonies. "I also have become as you are." Why would they now embrace a religious viewpoint he had rejected in light of Christ's having made such rituals meaningless, as expressed above?

B. Received without Reservation (vv. 10–15)

Paul points to the Galatians' generous receptivity of his person even though he appeared in great weakness and physical need (vv. 13–14). The false apostles had called him a "man-pleaser" who was persuasive only because of certain manipulative tactics. In chapter 1, he pointed out his intense confrontation with them as evidence that he had no desire to win his way among them by "trying to please man" (v. 10).

1. Here he reminds them that they received him initially despite his physical weakness, even his dependency. They did him no wrong, even though they could easily have taken advantage of his sickness.

2. He did not come in strength but was among them only because a bodily illness forced him to remain there. Amid his weakness, he preached the gospel to them (v. 13).

3. It seems that Paul's condition was so severe that his presence could have been seen as a real imposition, and caring for him cost them both time and energy and perhaps some monetary expense. Had he been trying to win them by power, personality, and subtle zeal, his sojourn with them was most unpropitious for his purpose.

4. Instead, however, they seemed immediately to understand the transcendent value of his presence with them. His sickness was nothing compared to the treasure of truth he spoke to them.

C. Paul's Particular Language (vv. 13–15)

Note Paul's language about his work and their reception of it: "preached the gospel"; "an angel of God"; "as Christ Jesus"; "the blessing you felt."

1. When a bodily illness made him seek rest among them, nevertheless, he "preached the gospel" (v. 13). This message so captured their thought (at least at that time) that they considered his weakness as insignificant in comparison with the character of the truth he proclaimed, inscribing before them that "Jesus Christ was publicly portrayed as crucified" (3:1).

2. They did not see him as a burden to tolerate but as "an angel" or special messenger "of God." However they envisioned him now, at that time—when they had the most reason to doubt his value—his preaching convinced them he was from God.

3. In addition, there was no ambivalence to his message. So alive was he to the gospel and its historical reality and spiritual necessity as arising from Jesus Christ and Him only, that they knew he was not there for himself but for Christ. So, they received him not as a sick siphon on their lives but as the presence of the Savior Himself. They experienced what Paul meant when he wrote to the Philippians: "For to me to live is Christ" (1:21), and also to them: "It is no longer I who live, but Christ who lives in me" (Gal. 2:20).

4. Paul reminded them of the sense of blessing that they had. When they learned of the true and living God, learned of the forgiveness of sins, and saw in Christ the true revelation of God in His intent to save, they felt the reality of the blessedness of those graces. Now he asks them, "What then has become of your blessedness?" (v. 15).

5. In fact, the sense of blessing made all appearance of earthly weakness seem as nothing, and any cost to meet the needs of Paul would not have been too much. Their grasp of the eternal advantages of the gospel made all temporal things as nothing. They even would have pulled out their eyes and given them to Paul in light of the advantage they had gained from his message.

6. His proclamation of the truth brought them eternal gain and endeared him to them. Now that he continues with a message of truth in his warning, is he considered an enemy (v. 16)?

Sylvia's Comments (vv. 12–15)

After throwing up his hands in despair, Paul reminds them of how much he cares, using the words "brothers," and "entreat." He asks them to "look at me," because in Christ we are the same. He makes a personal plea, speaking from his heart, recounting their first experience together. They cared for him when he was sick, and he gave them the gospel. Their relationship grew strong through crisis, and hopefully they will get through this with an even stronger tie. Evidently, caring for him was hard and maybe contagious, but they honored him as if Christ were with them. They were so concerned and happy to serve him, they sacrificed whatever was necessary for his benefit. He gave them an even greater benefit by preaching the gospel.

III. Zeal for the Galatians; Devotion Can Be Good and Bad (4:17–20)

A. Eager False Teachers (v. 17)

The new teachers were working hard to gain the attention of the Christians in Galatia.

1. They eagerly are courting the Galatians' favor, but not in a commendable way. If these teachers were seeking to help them grow in the grace and understanding of the gospel, Paul would be urging the Galatians to listen to them (as he does so in 1 Cor. 16:10–16).

2. Instead, they want to discredit the gospel in its freeness to the Gentiles, thereby shutting them out. They would argue that Paul was not telling them the whole truth. There were things he had not let them know, and, therefore, they did not yet have the blessings brought by the Messiah. Certainly, therefore, the Galatian Christians would want these teachers to make up for what was lacking: "They wish to shut you out so that you will seek them" (v. 17 NASB95).

B. Zeal Commended (v. 18)

Paul commended the zeal of others in a good cause. It is a good thing when teachers are eager to impart truth that will edify the hearer. This kind of zeal to be heard and to engage other Christians in discussions of truth for their growth is commendable.

1. This is what Paul told the Romans he desired for them: "For I long to see you, that I may impart to you some spiritual gift to strengthen you" (Rom. 1:11). Paul wanted the Galatians to be well-taught by other true teachers, even when he was not with them. He knew that God distributed gifts of edification according to His own determination, but the truthfulness of the gift must be tested in light of its relation to the sole sufficiency and absolute effectuality of the work of Christ (see also 1 Cor. 3:10–15).

2. The further teaching in the "gospel" must not contradict prior revelation they had received from Paul's faithful labors among them.

C. Paul's Anguish (v. 19)

Unlike the false teachers who were zealous for the Galatians for their own gain, Paul feels a deep sense of pain for them for the sake of Christ.

He feels as if he must go through the entire birth process again to see them born into the kingdom, "for whom I am again in the anguish of childbirth until Christ is formed in you."

D. Paul's Perplexity (v. 20)

If Paul were with them in person, he could see and sense their response and engage in some immediate response. In such a situation, he would change his tone. But as he only has the medium of the written word without the advantage of seeing their faces, hearing their questions, and urging them with tenderness (1 Thess. 2:5–8), he must stay the course in his stern warning about the dangerous precipice of error they are approaching. The entire phenomenon is perplexing to Paul.

Sylvia's Comments (vv. 16–20)

After recounting their friendship forged in Christ and crisis, he asks if he is now the enemy. If so, then the truth is their enemy also. These false teachers are flattering and praising them, but their intent is evil—for no good reason. In fact, the goal is to put them under the law and under their thumbs. Paul wants to compliment and praise the Galatian Christians for good reasons—holding to the gospel—but he can't. As a mother goes through the pain of childbirth for the joy of nurturing her child, Paul is willing to go through this painful time to see Christ formed in his "little children." As they sacrificed during his illness to care for him, Paul will sacrifice to protect them from evil. He would love to be there to look them in their eyes, touch them, and talk face to face. Maybe then he could take away the confusion.

IV. The Issue: Is the Gospel a Message of True Freedom or of Continued Enslavement? (4:21–31)

A. The Line of Bondage (vv. 21–25)

In the last eleven verses of this chapter, Paul draws two

analogies, beginning with Abraham in both. In one, he traces the line of bondage.

1. Paul's line runs from Ishmael, Abraham's son by Hagar the slave woman; Mount Sinai; and the Jews of Jerusalem still caught in the bondage of the entire Mosaic legal code. Ishmael arose from the attempt to fulfill the promise of God by human power; it was an action of the flesh.

2. That is the way of bondage and keeps one under the curse of the law. The covenant with God is seen to depend on human works. It promotes a perverted vision both of human goodness and the nature of God's promise. It establishes a debt to the ceremonial and moral law for righteousness that can never be paid. Moreover, it depends on the perverse strength of the flesh for its fulfillment—an impossibility, for the "desires of the flesh are against the Spirit" (5:17).

3. All this is impossible and makes slaves of its adherents. To this bondage, the false teachers invited the Gentiles of Galatia.

Sylvia's Comments (vv. 21–25)

Paul approaches the problem from a different angle. He asks if they want to be under the law and then tells them to look the law in the face through Hagar and Sarah. He contrasts them: Hagar was a slave, Sarah was free. Hagar's son was a result of the flesh, while Sarah's son was born because of God's promise. He goes on to compare Hagar with slavery under the law as given on Mount Sinai and to the earthly Jerusalem in its constraints.

B. The Line of Freedom (vv. 26–31)

The second analogy traces the son of freedom, Isaac. This line is the line of freedom.

1. He completes the analogy by extending a line from Isaac, the son of promise born of Sarah the free woman, all the way to the Jerusalem above, the home of the children of promise.

2. This line produces the children of promise, conceived in the joy of divine promise, and produces true children of God, whereas the children of the flesh do not produce one child of God (v. 27). The Galatians are analogous to Isaac's "children of promise" (v. 28).

3. Even as Ishmael mocked Isaac (Gen. 21:9), so the Judaizers mock those who receive the promise of Abraham and put no confidence in the flesh. They seek to draw the sons of promise back to bondage as sons of the flesh. The Judaizers mock the way of life by promise and want to draw free people into the strictures of their bondage. The one is born of the flesh, the other of the Spirit.

4. The Scripture presents another detail of the analogy from Genesis 21:10, 12 that the child of the flesh was cast out so as not to be an heir with the son of promise. Even so, the Galatian Christians, the recipients of Paul's gospel of free and pure grace, should not forsake their inheritance since they are "an heir through God" (Gal. 4:7) but should separate themselves from these teachers of bondage. They are children of the free woman, justified freely, received as sons, released from the curse, and receivers of a glorious inheritance.

Sylvia's Comments (vv. 27–31)

Sarah corresponds with the heavenly Jerusalem that is ours because of faith and the promise of God. She was desolate and then had one child. But God has blessed the nations through that one child by keeping His word and sending Christ to redeem His people. In Christ, we are brothers and children of promise and live in freedom. But just as Ishmael persecuted Isaac, be aware there always will be people who want to bring us down again. Do not listen to them. Walk away. Turn away those who are persecuting you by trying to steal your inheritance and enslave you.

Chapter 7

All We Need Is Love

Galatians 5

This chapter is an exposition of the freedom of the Christian. The child of God is free from the impossible task of being justified by his own works of the law (although the law's demand for perfect righteousness has not ceased) and from its curse. He is free to express the law's call for love in the power of the Spirit with no fear of condemnation from its imperfections.

I. The Liberty by Which We Are Free (5:1–6)

Paul begins by affirming and defining the particular liberty by which we are free.

A. Set Free from the Demands of the Law (v. 1)

Christ set us free from the immutable legal demands of the law so we would not be bound either by its curse or by its requirement of unalloyed perfection in obedience

(v. 1). For freedom from this damning lordship of the law, Christ has set us free by His own perfect work. Paul admonished the Galatians, therefore, to stand firm in the gospel he has taught them and not allow other teachers to reimpose the law on them.

Sylvia's Comments (v. 1)

As a twenty-first-century American Christian, sometimes I forget how horrid slavery is. It's not in my face day in and day out. I live in a country where freedom is valued and slavery was a festering sore for years, whose scar is slowly fading away. I know I don't want to be an earthly slave, but there is an infinitely greater slavery. The law's slavery is unendingly oppressive. The New Testament indicates that anyone, slave or free, who receives the gospel is free in Christ.

Paul is saying that by adding the law to make us right with God, we are snapping on the bonds of slavery again. We are freed by Christ from the bondage of the law, and we are to stand unwaveringly on the solid rock of faith.

B. Circumcision Implied the Entire Legal Code (vv. 2–4)

Circumcision was the first and most identifiable aspect of the ceremonial requirements of the law. It has been fulfilled through the work of Christ in His bloody sacrifice and in sending His Spirit to give believers a circumcision of heart (Col. 2:11). Thus, first, to submit to a ritual, the meaning of which has been consummated in the finished redemption, is to prefer the shadow to the substance, and Christ will be of no benefit. To receive circumcision would be to reject Christ as Redeemer. One would, as it were, substitute a picture of Christ for Christ Himself.

Second, to receive circumcision would be to embrace the ceremonial law as necessary for salvation (v. 3). If the ceremonial law is necessary for salvation, how much more would fulfillment of the moral law be necessary? So, if one consents to circumcision, he, in effect, puts himself back under the demands of the moral law which involves a curse (3:10).

And third, one may find righteousness in the law by his own perfect fulfillment of it, or he may find it in Christ by His perfect fulfillment of it (v. 4). To receive one's own fulfillment of any aspect of the law as necessary for salvation severs one from Christ and substitutes our obedience for the obedience of Christ. In this way, one would be severed from Christ and dependent on works, not on grace. But we are "justified by faith in Christ and not by the works of the law, because by works of the law no one will be justified" (Gal. 2:16); rather, "by grace you have been saved through faith" (Eph. 2:8).

Sylvia's Comments (vv. 2–4)

Paul is reminding us that if we add even one requirement of the law to justify us before God, we must keep the whole law. Christ kept the whole law, not just circumcision. Is my obedience better than Christ's? Before I believed, I didn't keep the law. None of us did. And now, having been severed from living as a slave to the flesh, sin, and the law,

> I actually put on the chains of slavery by adding even one item to my to-do list. I am not living by faith anymore, so Christ's sacrifice means nothing. I no longer am living in the grace of God by faith in Christ, I am depending on my own obedience.

C. The Hope of Righteousness (vv. 5–6)

The hope that salvation gives is not in our own righteousness but that received by faith. The way God gives salvation is absolutely contrary to the message preached by the Judaizers.

1. First, we know we have been brought into the awareness of sin and salvation by the work of the Spirit. The Spirit takes the gospel, opens our hearts to see the glory of Christ and His righteousness, and works faith in us. "For through the Spirit, by faith, we ourselves eagerly wait for the hope of righteousness" (v. 5).

2. The "hope of righteousness" means the confidence that we have in being with Christ forever comes from trusting in the perfection of His righteousness. We may stand in the presence of God in the enjoyment of His happiness and beauty only in the clothing of perfect righteousness. This is granted to us by faith, and faith is the result of the special operations of the Spirit of God.

3. In Christ, the distinction between Jew and Gentile established by circumcision has been abolished (v. 6). The only difference it ever made was to maintain the identity of a covenant people who had been chosen as the nation through whom the Messiah would come.

The Messiah was always promised as one through whom the nations would be blessed. Thus, Paul makes the radical statement, "In Christ Jesus neither circumcision nor uncircumcision counts for anything."

4. The full intent of the law, therefore, is established in "faith working through love" (v. 6).

- Faith as a Christian grace uniquely unites the sinner to Christ in His full saving work. The entire mental and spiritual apparatus of faith perfectly coincides with the provision of Jesus Christ for forgiveness and righteousness.

- But even behind faith is the Spirit-born reality of love. Those truths to which faith consents could not be embraced unless love had been laid as a foundation in the soul. The Ten Commandments are all about loving God and loving man. We will not repent of sin if we do not affirm the true loveliness of God's law, both in its presentation of the duty to worship, honor, and serve God and its requirement that we place the same value on the well-being and happiness of our neighbor as we place on ours. We will not place faith in Christ if we do not give heartfelt consent to the lovely way in which He alone has met all the righteous, holy, and beautiful precepts of the law.

- So, love does not save, for our love is as yet imperfect and does not constitute righteousness, but it does give the disposition to approve all that the law requires and leads us to embrace Christ as the only one in whom God can justly receive us into eternal life. Thus, no merely external conformity to ceremonial law can do us any good at all but only "faith working through love."

- Paul affirms the same experiential reality in 6:15 where he writes, in his own hand, "For neither circumcision counts for anything, nor uncircumcision." The next phrase, having a parallel meaning with "faith working through love," is "but a new creation." Paul gives the same force then to these phrases. The regenerative work of the Holy Spirit in giving a new moral direction in conformity to the intent of the law precedes faith. This new moral perception convinces us of sin, righteousness, and judgment (John 16:8–11) so that we throw the entire weight of our needy souls on the finished work of Christ.

Sylvia's Comments (vv. 5–6)

Paul keeps pounding home the only way for redemption. Through the Spirit, we have real hope. Keeping our eyes focused on the truth, joyfully anticipating the fulfillment of our hope, we will be like Christ. Only faith working through love counts to that end. Nothing else counts. Our accounts are already declared "paid in full." Nothing can be added to increase our standing with God—and nothing can be taken away to decrease that standing.

II. Damning Consequences (5:7–12)

There are damning consequences in following the

wrong person and adopting the wrong persuasion. In verse 1, Paul used the image of "standing firm." Here he changes the picture and speaks of their "running well" (v. 7).

A. A Fatal Hindrance (v. 7)

In the midst of their running well, someone has "hindered" them "from obeying the truth" (v. 7). Paul refers to this person with several disturbing ideas. Paul uses a term to which he will return later. This person has, in essence, cut them off from the truth.

1. This is a person who has given them a system in opposition to the truth. Not only has he proposed an alternative way of being rightly related to God but also has sought to convince them that Paul's message has no exclusive claim to be true.

2. The message is one of pure fleshly power, not of the work of the Spirit. The Spirit's work is to draw the sinner to Christ; this person has contradicted the Spirit's work by making them focus on their conformity to ceremonial law.

3. This person is disturbing the Christians of Galatia, bringing about confusion, seeking to move them to another view. In so doing, he will bring judgment on himself. These truths are matters of eternal life and eternal death. As in the first chapter Paul issued "anathema" on those who preached a gospel other than the one he preached, so here he points to this person as coming to a time when he will bear his judgment. The judgment could be church discipline,

but Paul seems to point to the final judgment in which he will be condemned as an unjustified person and his punishment will be exacerbated by his having led others astray.

B. Ideas Matter (vv. 8–10)

Paul refers to this alternative message in light of the message he preached (vv. 8–10).

1. He calls his message "the truth." The person disturbing them sought to forestall their believing the truth.

2. He calls the false message a "persuasion" (v. 8). The ceremonialist had mounted an argument to drive them from one position on salvation to another. Paul's truth found effectuality through "Him who calls you" (v. 8). To this work of the Spirit Paul also appealed in his first letter to the Corinthian church: "And my speech and my message were not in plausible words of wisdom, but in demonstration of the Spirit and of power" (1 Cor. 2:4).

3. If this false teacher has succeeded to any degree, then all is lost, for "a little leaven leavens the whole lump" (v. 9). In the matter of justification, the admission of even the slightest aspect of human conformity to the law alters the entire doctrine and drives Christ away. There is no halfway compromise between Paul's message of justification by faith and this attempt at performance religion.

4. Paul expresses confidence that they would recognize the fallacy of this alternative religion, would adopt "no other view" (v. 10), no other manner of thinking.

Throughout this faceoff of ideas, Paul recedes not the slightest from his argument of the revelatory character of the gospel he preached but continues his insistence on its absolutely truthful manifestation of God's way of justifying sinners.

Sylvia's Comments (vv. 7–9)

The Galatians' Christian journey is compared to a race in which they were doing very well but something got in the way. They were obeying the truth, and someone tripped them, but it wasn't God. Paul then reminds them that a small amount of yeast works through the whole lump of dough. Saying that one little law is necessary for justification opens the floodgates to keeping the whole law.

C. False Teachers, False Claims (vv. 10–12)

They made a false claim about Paul, saying that even he recognized circumcision was intrinsic to being God's people. Outraged at the lie, Paul issues another malediction toward the false teacher—he "will bear the penalty, whoever he is" (v. 10).

1. The false teachers claimed that even Paul returned to circumcision when he had Timothy circumcised (Acts 16:3). For Paul, this was not connected to his message of the gospel at all but was purely a pragmatic action so that Timothy could go with Paul into Jewish synagogues to witness the nature of gospel dialogue in a hostile environment.

2. "If I . . . still preach circumcision" (v. 11).

- He had done this before during the days when he persecuted, but now he himself is being persecuted, and that by the circumcision party. If he preached circumcision, they would not persecute him.

- The offense of the cross would be gone, and the Jews would no longer oppose him (see also 1 Cor. 1:23 —"but we preach Christ crucified, a stumbling block to Jews and folly to Gentiles, but to those who are called, both Jews and Greeks, Christ the power of God and the wisdom of God"). Here again, we find Paul's distinction between persuasion, or human wisdom, and the call generated by God's power.

- Since these false teachers tried to "cut off" the Galatians from the truth, why don't they just cut themselves off (v. 12)? He could be referring to the image of circumcision and mean that they should simply emasculate themselves. He could mean that, instead of cutting off others from the truth, they should cut themselves off from any connection with the "Jesus is Messiah" movement. They do not advance the cause of Christ or increase reverence for Him but only make His work unnecessary. Jesus is Messiah only if the cross is effectual.

Sylvia's Comments (vv. 10–12)

Paul strikes a hopeful note. Despite this perplexing situation, he knows they will hear the truth and obey because he has confidence in the Lord. Nothing will ever separate those who are in Christ Jesus from His love. God will also deal with whoever is trying to dissuade them from living by faith. Verse 11 seems to indicate the false teachers may have said, "This is what Paul is teaching." Paul says, "No way!" On the one hand, they try to discredit Paul; on the other, they say, "This is even what he believes." Paul suggests that these false teachers don't stop at circumcision but go on to emasculate themselves as the pagans do.

III. Another Look at Freedom and Living by the Spirit (5:13–26)

A. *Faith Works through Love (v. 13–15)*

Here Paul expands on the idea that faith works through love. Freedom from the law's condemnation and freedom from the necessity of achieving the merit of eternal life through our own obedience (impossible) does not mean that the moral profile of the law is rendered irrelevant. When Paul asked in Romans 3:31, "Do we then overthrow the law by this faith?" he answered, "By no means! On the contrary, we uphold the law."

And here, Paul seems to use the word "flesh" in a different way.

1. In the first instance, he used the term to indicate human works in an attempt to achieve righteousness by personal endeavor (3:3; 4:23).

2. Here he is speaking of the flesh as a principle of opposition to godliness and given over to the pursuit

of pleasure and preeminence arising from the idolatry of self.

- This is seen in the positive admonition Paul gives: "Through love serve one another" (v. 13).

- Since faith arises from love, we see that true faith will seek ways to show its exalted view of the law: "For the whole law is fulfilled in one word: 'You shall love your neighbor as yourself'" (v. 14). Here he is writing about the second table of the law, working from the principle that he who does not love his neighbor cannot love God.

- On the other hand, unmortified selfishness will destroy the entire fellowship: "If you bite and devour one another, watch out that you are not consumed by one another" (v. 15). By love, we are to serve one another, not destroy one another through selfishness. "The Son of Man came not to be served but to serve, and to give his life as a ransom for many" (Mark 10:45). Indwelling sin can poison personal relationships with such subtlety and self-justification that we sometimes think we're acting with a sense of personal integrity and courage when we're actually working to destroy the spiritual comfort and well-being of others.

Sylvia's Comments (vv. 13–15)

Paul adds to his letter by encouraging them to think about who they are in Christ. He points out our freedom is in Christ and, through it, our ability to love as God loves. Our freedom is freedom to serve, to give, to sacrifice for others, to love God and call Him *Father*. Christ summed up the law in two commandments: love God first and your neighbor as yourself. In John 15:12, He tells the disciples to love one another as He loved them. God enables us to love Him and others because His basic nature is love. When we act selfishly, proudly, or spitefully, we are acting in opposition to God. The outcome of this will be very ugly.

C. Walking by the Spirit (vv. 16–26)

Even as the Spirit is set in opposition to the flesh in the matter of justification by faith, so the Spirit is set in opposition to the flesh in the matter of sanctification, or growing in Christlikeness.

1. Walk by the Spirit to not gratify the desires of the flesh (v. 16). One may trace out Paul's emphasis on the Spirit up to this point (3:2–3, 5, 14; 4:6, 29; 5:5). Your life now, Paul implies, is a manifestation of the presence of the Spirit if you have indeed been brought to trust Christ.

- He has inspired the word of truth by which we learn the gospel (1 Peter 1:11–12; 2 Peter 1:20–21).

- He has sovereignly granted the new birth (John 3:1–8).

- He has indwelt us as the Spirit of sonship (Gal. 4:6).

- He resides in us as a sanctifying power (Rom. 8:14).

- He grants gifts so that the whole body grows in grace and knowledge (1 Cor. 12; Eph. 4:1–13; 1 Peter 4:8–11).

Sylvia's Comments (vv. 16–18)

Because we are redeemed and no longer enslaved to our sin nature, we are able to walk by the Spirit. Adam and Eve were able to walk daily with God before the fall. But sin blocked that open relationship, and it was not restored until Christ tore down the wall. Now, by faith, we don't have to obey our sin nature. We are free to live by the Spirit, set free from the law. Paul knows we can still choose to sin, so he warns us: sin is the opposite of righteousness; the flesh fights against the Spirit. Christians want to obey God but still must actively put the flesh (sin nature) to death.

---

2. Walking in the Spirit will produce an unending conflict with the flesh until we are freed from its presence in heaven. In this conflict, we should know how to evaluate the variety of affections and desires that arise. If we have a firm grasp on the nature of the flesh, we can recognize those works as they operate, seeking to destroy us:

- Paul first mentions three perversions of sexuality: "sexual immorality, impurity, sensuality" (v. 18). These kinds of sins are the most widespread and indicate the immediate impulse of the flesh to seek personal sensual pleasure without regard to the will of the Creator. They include fornication,

homosexuality, orgiastic living, and the sexualiz-
ing of society through pornography, provocative
advertisement, entertainment, and formal arguments for celebration of alternative sexualities.
We must not recede from the biblical pattern of
sexuality, either in personal living, in corporate
holiness in the church, in proclamation, or in
our arguments in the marketplace of ideas. Paul
described in Romans 1:24–32 how perverted sexuality is one of the most obvious and early manifestations of the lawlessness of fallen humanity,
opening the door for aggressive violation of the
entire moral code of the Ten Commandments.
God does not whisper about sexual sin, but he
shouts loudly and with fatal warning.

- Second, Paul uses two words for false religion:
"idolatry" and "sorcery" (v. 20). Idolatry is the bla-
tant substitution of deities of human imagination
for the one true God. Sorcery (Gr. *Pharmakeia*)
points to the efforts to engender religious experience through magical potions and incantations.
In these instances, religion does not involve worship of the one true God but is an effort to seek
alternate ways of quieting a disturbed soul.

- Third, Paul uses eight words that focus on the internal attitudes and aggressions that tend toward division, conflict, prejudice, anger, revenge, grudges,
and acquisitiveness. These show that interpersonal
relationships are corrupted (vv. 20–21).

- Fourth, these works of the flesh corrupt social
order (v. 21). Drunkenness and carousing

create instability and danger in social settings and indulge an attempt to gain personal pleasure and the power of intimidation at the expense of the common good. There is no such thing as a funny drunk, only a pitiful, sad perversion of human dignity and an attack on the order, symmetry, beauty, and rationality of the image of God in humanity. There is no such thing as a "good ol' time" in carousing but only an idolatrous substitution of pleasure-centered living for finding one's pleasure in the knowledge of God.

3. If we know the fruit of the Spirit, we can trust that He will supply the energy and power for that (vv. 22–23). These are the "normal outcropping of the Holy Spirit in us" (A. T. Robertson). Knowing this, we also can seek to inculcate those holy actions and attitudes distinctly expressive of the divine nature (see also 2 Peter 1:4–10, where Peter admonishes his readers to "be all the more diligent").

- Since "fruit" is singular and the list begins with "love," Paul probably is using that word as inclusive of all the qualities that follow. Earlier he wrote that faith works through love. Then he writes that love is the fulfillment of the law (v. 14), and here Paul concludes the list by affirming "against such things there is no law" (v. 23). In his first letter to Timothy, Paul writes that the goal of his instruction is "love that issues from a pure heart and a good conscience and a sincere faith" (1:5).

- Paul's discussion of love in 1 Corinthians 13 includes, in a variety of ways, the same ideas expressed here. He contrasts love with works of the flesh, to which one may find parallels in the list in Galatians 5: "Love ... does not envy or boast [vs. jealousy]; is not arrogant, or rude. It does not insist on its own way; is not irritable [vs. strife, fits of anger, rivalries], or resentful [vs. disputes]; it does not rejoice at wrongdoing [vs. immorality, etc.]" (1 Cor. 13:4–6).

- Positive parallels also exist such as love is patient (patience), kind (kindness), rejoices in the truth (joy), bears all things (patience), believes all things (faith as the fruit of love), endures all things (patience and self-control).

- Since the law seeks to promote every spiritual fruit listed here, obviously, unlike the works of the flesh, there is no law against them. Freedom from the curse of the law through the work of Christ embraced through the power of the Spirit does not establish a path to lawlessness but promotes the true godliness intended by the law.

Sylvia's Comments (vv. 19–23)

The works of the flesh are all around us, and we need to recognize them as evil. To continue to practice or excuse sin is a sign we are not headed toward the kingdom of God. Paul has warned the Galatians and warns them—and us—again about professing Christ and living like the devil. Spiritual fruit is summed up in verses 22 and 23. As we study Christ, we see these qualities. Through Scripture meditation, prayer, and being washed with the

Word through preaching, teaching, and reading, we become more like Christ. We shed the old sinful passions and desires and cover ourselves with the wholeness of Christ. The law cannot provide these qualities, but they are ours through faith in Christ.

---

4. "Those who belong to Christ have crucified the flesh with its passions and desires" (v. 24). This is a summary of the whole of the Christian life.

5. "If we live by the Spirit" (v. 25).

- The desire of the prideful flesh for achieving merit and acceptance on the basis of personal worth has been crucified by seeing in Christ our only hope for righteousness and eternal life. In this way, we live by the Spirit. The same regenerative work of the Spirit that produced repentance from sin and faith in Christ did so by contradicting the demands of the corrupt heart and establishing a love of righteousness. We trust Christ and love him for he is the righteous One. If this work of the Spirit had not occurred first, no one would repent and believe.

- "Let us also keep in step with the Spirit" (v. 25). The flesh, in its grasp for pleasure in fulfilling its lusts, has been crucified by the Spirit's placing Christ before us in the beauty of His holiness. Since the life of the soul and the promise of eternal life have come through the Spirit's effectual work of uniting us to Christ by faith, we should continue to walk in the same spiritual impulse that led us to Christ.

6. Paul gives a summarized warning about the subtleties of the flesh in warning against becoming conceited (v. 26). This is an attitude that increases provocation to jealousy and envy. The following chapter gives instruction as to how, within the church, we may help one another in this vital pursuit of walking in the Spirit.

Sylvia's Comments (vv. 25–26)

The Spirit gives you life, so let your life show the Spirit. Alert! Don't look down on one another. Don't compare your Christian journey with someone else's. Be content with what God has given you and where you are. Remember, God judges man by his heart, not his "looks." We are to be peacemakers, not troublemakers.

Chapter 8

The Brand Marks of Jesus

Galatians 6

I. Be Humble and Helpful, Not Conceited and Self-Absorbed (6:1–5)

Paul shows how, in contrast to 5:26, the individual should relate to his fellow Christians. As we walk by the Spirit, we will not seek superiority over another or try to destroy the usefulness of another, but we will seek their usefulness and their spiritual growth and health in all things.

A. Restoring a Transgressing Member (v. 1)

When a sin of the flesh becomes obvious in an individual so that the church recognizes its destructive tendency, a process of restoration should be pursued.

1. The scene here is not that a person has planned and contrived to trespass God's law but that the energy of the flesh has arisen in light of a sudden temptation that, combined with the subtlety of the flesh, has caught him or her. This seemingly could involve a lapse into any of the sins of the flesh described in chapter 5: an outburst of anger that causes hurt and division, absence from worship to pursue other activities, inability to control an appetite for wine, sexual indiscretion, or unfaithfulness, or nursing a jealous or envious spirit toward a fellow church member whose gifts might give him or her public prominence. Upon the discovery of a pattern of any of these, the goal is to restore such a person to an awareness of the danger and power of the flesh and help them "walk by the Spirit." Some of these might involve discipline, others only admonition and instruction, but all are pitfalls that call for rescue. In each case, the restorer must remember that "a soft answer turns away wrath, but a harsh word stirs up anger" (Prov. 15:1). At the same time, this admonition is built on the confidence that "whoever heeds reproof is prudent," but "whoever hates reproof will die" (Prov. 15:5, 10).

2. When this occurs, the task of the brethren, therefore, is to restore, not destroy, the person. Those who may be gifted at spiritual counsel and are seeking consciously to walk in the Spirit, as per 5:25, should undertake this restoration. The restoration will involve recognition, repentance, and resolution.

- *Recognition of the sinfulness of the trespass.* The

person is aware of and acknowledges that his action has violated a commandment of God.

- *Repentance from the sin.* The person is remorseful to the point of genuine sorrow that God has been dishonored by his action, and he is determined to turn from the sin and renew his guard against such sudden and unwatchful failure.

- *Resolution to live by the Spirit.* His deeper knowledge of the sinful fragility of his flesh will give firmness to his resolution to inculcate the fruit of the Spirit so as to avoid works of the flesh.

3. This restoration must be saturated with a spirit of gentleness, not repression, superiority, or even rejoicing in the weakness and fall of another. The restorers must see themselves as fellow sinners and as liable to fall should they be left to their own strength. When they see the way in which another was overtaken with the war of the flesh, the restorers must examine their own hearts and be warned that the devil and the flesh are not respecters of persons but will assault one as well as another. In fact, the more upright the target appears, the more prone to the fiery darts of the evil one.

B. Shouldering Another's Burden (v. 2)

We must help shoulder the burdens of fellow Christians. Their road to recovery, not the promotion of their shame, should be the central concern of those who have been deemed spiritually qualified to work in the process of restoration. Christ bore our burdens, and when He asked us to take His yoke on ourselves, He pointed to Himself as "gentle and lowly in heart," and taught that the yoke was not designed to increase the burden but to lighten it for it is designed to give rest to our souls (Matt. 11:25–30).

C. Restoration Apart from Recrimination (v. 3)

The process of restoration and the shouldering of the burdens of others must not result in a spirit of superiority. If we believe we have not fallen because we are less affected by sin than others or we have greater moral fiber, we become like the Pharisee who thanked God that he was not like other men (Luke 18:10–14). In ourselves, we are nothing and can do nothing (John 15:4–5). Matthew Henry observed that the one who so thinks "is neither the freer from mistakes nor will he be the more secure against temptations for the good opinion he has of his own sufficiency, but rather the more liable to fall into them and to be overcome by them."

D. A Satisfying Sense of Faithfulness (vv. 4–5)

We gain a sense of satisfaction before God, not by comparison to others, but by a deep awareness of being a steward of gifts and opportunities and faithfulness in calling.

1. We do not judge our standing by the failure of others but by personal conformity to the Word of God. "Let each one test his own work" (v. 4). He must look at it carefully so as to find it done genuinely in the spirit of Christ and for the glory of God. He looks at it to test and see if it conforms to God's calling and gifting to him. If one can see that, by God's grace (Gal.

2:8), benefits have come to others through effectual labors, "then his reason to boast will be in himself alone and not in [the failings of] his neighbor" (v. 4).

2. Paul applied this principle to the apostles and those gifted persons who labored with zeal during the apostolic period. By the kindness of God and His zeal for His glory, much of that work will be seen as "gold, silver, precious stones." Some will be "wood, hay, straw." All of it "will become manifest, for the Day will disclose it, because it will be revealed by fire, and the fire will test what sort of work each one has done" (1 Cor. 3:12–13). The key there, even as in Galatians, is that the foundation of all of this is Jesus Christ. All that is consistent with His person and work and promotes faith in Him will not be destroyed; all that is inconsistent with that standard, whether for justification or sanctification, will be destroyed.

3. Even in his most candid moments of transparent faithfulness, Paul knew his heart had hidden recesses of pollution that tainted his best actions and deceived his most lucid judgments (see 1 Cor. 4:1–5). "I am not aware of anything against myself, but I am not thereby acquitted. It is the Lord who judges me. Therefore do not pronounce judgment before the time, before the Lord comes, who will bring to light the things now hidden in darkness and will disclose the purposes of the heart. Then each one will receive his commendation from God" (vv. 4–5).

Sylvia's Comments (vv. 1–5)

More encouragement and admonition from Paul. If you see sin in a brother or sister, help them! Gently, compassionately help them find restoration to the truth. Sin is a burden, and we are coming to their aid to get rid of it and bring them back to living by the Spirit. Always keep in mind that we are all vulnerable, and treat them as you would want to be treated. The fruit of the Spirit should guide all our interactions, even when dealing with someone's sin. Don't pat yourself on the back when all is said and done. Check out your own attitudes, desires, intents. Live humbly, don't flaunt your good works, carry your own backpack, and take responsibility for your own issues.

II. Paul Looks at Spirituality and Money (6:6–10)

As we work to restore the "overtaken" (v. 1 NKJV) on a case-by-case basis, so the church should make sure it receives instruction regularly in the revealed truth of God. It is by the searchlight of God's Word, the ever-unfolding implications of gospel truth, that we will be thoroughly "equipped for every good work" (2 Tim. 3:17).

A. On Not Muzzling the Ox (v. 6)

Those who have the task and calling of feeding the Word of God to the church should be supported in their earthly needs by the church. Paul, though he set no requirement of regular monetary support for his work as an apostle, taught that a church should support a gospel ministry among themselves (read 1 Corinthians 9). He gladly received help when provided, both to meet his needs and to fulfill the sense of stewardship and sacrifice in the lives of those who shared with him (Phil. 4:10–20).

B. Sowing and Reaping (vv. 7–8)

We show the values we have by how we put our earthly wealth to use. Spending money is like sowing seed.

1. How we spend our earthly wealth tells a story about our hearts. Jesus told the story of the unjust steward to show that material wealth invested strategically transforms relationships and may be used for eternal good. We may use the "unrighteous mammon" for the sake of achieving eternal ends (Luke 16:1–13 KJV).

2. If we are cheap and covetous concerning our monetary status and use it on increasing temporal comfort and pleasure, going far beyond ordinary daily needs, then we will reap only the passing, fleeting, and failing fascinations of this present life. When they are done, nothing substantial remains. It is like eating a "Bit-O-Honey"—sweet in the mouth but soon gone and forgotten. "The one who sows to his own flesh" (6:8) will from such sowing reap corruption, an increasing load of the world that passes away (1 John 2:15–17).

3. If we use monetary wealth to gain and sustain a true preacher of the gospel as Paul argues for in these verses, then we sow to the Spirit. In this way, that

which Jesus called "unrighteous mammon" becomes transformed for the purpose of the righteousness of the gospel. Thus, through hearing the Word, we will "from the Spirit reap eternal life." Wicked mammon, given to the Spirit's purpose in empowering the preached Word, becomes transformed into a steady diet of eternal truth. It has the power to bring salvation, ongoing transformation of heart into the character of heaven.

C. Sow to the Spirit (v. 9)

We must seek to support and encourage those efforts that produce spiritual fruit based on gospel truth. It is not necessarily the immediate and spectacular success but the quality of the work to which we pay heed. If we keep sowing to the Spirit, if we keep hearing the Word, if we keep restoring the fallen, if we keep watching ourselves and our doctrine, we will of the Spirit reap life everlasting.

D. Do Good to Everyone (v. 10)

In addition to supporting gospel ministry, we must find ways to "do good" for all people, but particularly for fellow believers. This too is a spiritual use of material wealth. When we honor the image of God in all men by seeking their well-being, especially those who are also believers in the gospel and lovers of Christ, we observe the spiritual purpose for which God created the world.

The Brand Marks of Jesus | 131

Sylvia's Comments (vv. 6–10)

Paul covers some basics here:

- If you are being taught and shepherded, share with your teachers. Sharing all good things doesn't just mean financial support but expressing thankfulness, examples of blessings from your life, and results of the teaching in your life that are benefiting your work, neighborhood, school, etc.

- We can't fool God. He knows our hearts. If we are self-centered, doing things for show (hypocrisy), or are two-faced, we are feeding the flesh, which will destroy us. If we are looking to Christ, living by the Spirit, putting to death the flesh, we will enjoy our rich reward of unrestricted eternal life with God.

- Don't give up. We will get there if we surrender all to Christ.

- Look for opportunities to do good for others, especially other Christians.

III. Circumcision and the Cross (6:11–18)

A. A Letter Indeed Written by Paul (v. 11)

Paul closes the letter with his personal inscription. In light of the presence of false teaching and, at times, even false apostles, Paul wants the churches of Galatia to know that this hard-hitting message is indeed his own. His confidence in the gospel message he preached and his call as an apostle would work toward the eternal well-being of the recipients.

B. Works Righteousness Vs. Justification by Faith (vv. 12–16)

Paul summarizes his argument using the "flesh" as a principle of works righteousness and "the cross" as the principle of justification by faith.

1. Those who sought to impose the ceremonial law on the Gentiles were working to curry favor with the self-righteous who think that they are saved by their personal obedience to the law of Moses (v. 12). This concession is deadly to the gospel and is pursued only to avoid being persecuted for the cross. In 6:2, Paul referred to fulfilling the "law of Christ." Here he interprets our present obedience to the law in terms of pursuing the law of love, not for justification but for the sanctifying power of its focus on loving God and loving our neighbor.

2. The punctilious and fastidious attention to the ceremonial law of the Judaizers does not render them any less guilty as sinners before the law of God (v. 13). They, like all sons of Adam, as well as all sons of Abraham, are transgressors in need of justification outside of their own failed obedience. Though they do not keep the law, they believe that if they turn people back to the law of Moses as a way of approval before God, this will give them cause to boast. As Jesus said, "Woe to you, scribes and Pharisees, hypocrites! For you travel across sea and land to make a single proselyte, and when he becomes a proselyte, you make him twice as much a child of hell as yourselves" (Matt. 23:15). If the Galatians give in to them in even the slightest sense of achieving obedience

through the law, they will have forfeited all that is given in the cross.

3. Paul, therefore, does not boast in anyone's flesh (v. 14). Of the flesh we reap only corruption, death, and hell. He looks to the cross of Christ and all that it means in the complete fulfillment of the law. Both its curse (3:10, 13) and its relentless demand for righteousness (3:11–12) have been met in Christ and in Christ alone. This has completely transformed the vision of Paul, and he now looks to the eternal world where Christ is interceding for us while seated at the right hand of God (Col. 3:1–3; Heb. 1:3; 1 John 2:1–2). Paul has grasped the truth that we are made to live in the presence of God and enjoy His own happiness, joy in Himself, and the unalloyed love of heaven (2 Cor. 5:4–8; Phil. 3:10–14; John 17:24–26).

4. Circumcision is fulfilled in the sovereign work of the Holy Spirit in raising us from death to life, granting us the new birth and circumcision of the heart (v. 15, see also Eph. 2:1–4; John 3:3, 5; 6:61–65; Col. 2:12–13). The ceremony of circumcision has been fulfilled so that "neither circumcision counts for anything, nor uncircumcision." Instead, the new creation has taken the place of all the ceremonies, and Christ has bought for Himself a people. Those regenerated by the Spirit are now the "Israel of God." Upon them there is "peace and mercy" (v. 16). Those who grasp this truth, believe in the finality of the cross, and have received the Spirit of adoption constitute the people of God. They are the reconciled ones, thus having

peace. Theirs is the "God of peace who brought again
from the dead our Lord Jesus, the great shepherd of
the sheep" (Heb. 13:20). To them, God has been rich
in mercy. They are marked, not by circumcision but
by the fruit of the Spirit.

5. To this same truth, Peter witnesses in 1 Peter 2:4–10.
By the work of Christ applied by the Spirit, those
who were "not a people" now are a "chosen race, a
royal priesthood, a holy nation, a people for his own
possession" (v. 9). All who accounted Christ as worthy of rejection have forfeited the cornerstone. The
one, however, who does not "disobey the word," but
"believes in him" will have a new status. From being
"not a people," they have become "God's people."

Sylvia's Comments (vv. 14–16)

Paul boasts in Christ alone. He is clear on the point
that nothing can add to his justification. In Christ
he died to the world. Christ killed his and our sin
on the cross. Nothing matters in redemption but
the new creation in Christ. This is the only law, and
living by it is the way of peace and mercy for the
true Israel of God.

C. The Brand Marks of Jesus (v. 17)

Paul points not to circumcision of the flesh but to his
suffering for the cause of the gospel as the true marks of
Christian discipleship—on his body were "the brand-
marks of Jesus" (v. 17 NASB95).

Why should the sincerity of his work be questioned?

Why should the clarity of his theology of the cross be challenged? His very body testifies to both. Paul asks that he no longer have to engage this issue ("From now on let no one cause me trouble"), for his suffering for his message should be, to the Galatians, a sufficient witness to its truth.

D. A Profound Closing (v. 18)

Paul closes quickly but with a profound summary of the solution to this bothersome work with the Galatians. If they have been touched by saving grace, then all the components of their spirit will resonate with his message of justification. They will understand, believe, and love their acceptance before God through Christ alone by faith alone.

Sylvia's Comments (vv. 17–18)

If someone accuses Paul of faithlessness to the gospel, he bears the scars that came from faithfulness to Christ. Paul closes the letter showering his love on them with this benediction: grace in Christ to his brothers—and so it shall be.

Persuasives for Preaching and Piety

I. Paul's absolute certainty about the revelatory status of his gospel and all its implications should increase the clarity, energy, and confidence of our preaching (1:8, 12, 16). We stand to proclaim revealed truth, knowing its eternal relevance and that it separates light from darkness, truth from error, provides both cognition and motivation for godly living, and sets before mere mortals the glory of the One with whom we are designed to spend eternity.

II. Paul's argument concerning his apostleship should strengthen our commitment to the principle of *sola scriptura* and its implications (1:1; 2:5–7). The apostles were given to the church and commissioned by Christ to receive all necessary to make us wise unto salvation (2 Tim. 3:14–15) and to equip God's elect for all that pertains to life and godliness (2 Peter 1:2–4). We require no other revelation—should expect no other revelation—for the apostolic office, of which Paul appears to be the leading receptor and teacher, has concluded the revelation given by Jesus Christ (John 14:26; 15:20, 26; 16:12–15). Paul's strong insistence on his apostolic status finds verification in that his written contribution to the New Testament is 31 percent larger than that of the apostle John, and 62 percent of the book of Acts deals with the execution of his apostolic calling.

III. Paul's determination to please God, even when it meant suffering at the hands of men, should encourage us to love, speak, and practice the truth. Cutting through much of the rubbish of human opinion, pressure, and disdain, Paul encourages us all to live before God. In all lawful things we should seek to honor and please those who have positions of influence over us, but not at the expense of truth pursued in a faithful witness to the gospel (1:10; 5:11; 6:14).

IV. This letter should inform us of what it means to "contend for the faith that was once for all delivered to the saints" (Jude 3). Our message is one of finality and should be delivered earnestly and with a deep sense of what is at stake. Paul's doctrine determined eternity for those who heard with faith; alteration of its internal connections meant death (5:3–4).

V. Corresponding to that, we learn of the internal sense of fear, perplexity, and gnawing concern that afflicts the hearts and minds of pastors who realize that they must give an account for those under their teaching. The unmerited and unmeasured privilege and joy of handling revealed truth gives a corresponding sense of *gravitas* and compelling concern for those who will hear the message as preached (Gal. 4:11, 19–20; Heb. 13:17). "There is the daily pressure on me of my anxiety for all the churches" (2 Cor. 11:28).

VI. This letter should teach us how to embrace, in living and preaching, the absolutely gratuitous character of justification without fear that it will impede the sincere desire for transformation and substantial holiness (5:13). The law that makes necessary the one gives guidance to the other (Phil. 3:12).

VII. On the issue of law and gospel, this letter should demonstrate how the gospel does not initiate a new standard of righteousness above or distinct from the righteousness of the law. The gospel gives everything the law requires. The distinction between the moral and the ceremonial law runs as a theme throughout and shows that identifying the two is a deadly error (5:2).

VIII. Justification looks at the relevance of the *ceremonial law* as eliminated, for it was a temporal and typological pointer to substantial fulfillment in a person. This person, Jesus Christ, would bring those seasonal reminders of "not yet" to a complete end by their exuberant and superabounding fulfillment in His unblemished obedience (4:10; 5:6). Justification looks at the *moral law* as possessing eternal relevance. It establishes an absolute standard of righteousness, holding both a penalty and a promise (3:21). The penalty would be eternal death under condemnation, and the promise holds forth the hope of eternal life (5:4; 6:8; Titus 1:1, 2; 3:7).

IX. Sanctification also clearly delineates between the ceremonial and the moral law by its eschewing of the continuation of circumcision and its celebration of the holy standards of the moral law summarized in love (5:6). It would be inconsistent with the cumulative character of divine revelation for justification to come on the basis of any other standard of truth and righteousness than that revealed as the standard that would constitute righteousness and give life or, if disobeyed, would result in death (2:16, 19; 3:10, 13, 19, 21; 4:4–5). Even so, it would be inconsistent with the cumulative character of revelation for sanctification to look to any other standard than that which is revealed as the perfect standard of righteousness. This divinely given standard operates rightly only under the motivation of love, for moral perfection consists of incorruptible love to God and man (5:13–14; 1 Cor. 16:22).

X. Paul's argument shows the unifying aspect of the covenantal redemption decreed before the creation of the world. The covenant revealed to Abraham as operating on the basis of faith is a manifestation of Trinitarian wisdom and glory as revealed in the incarnation of the Son of God in His work for the people given Him by the Father and to be drawn to faith by the Spirit (3:14, 16–18, "the seed . . . to whom the promise had been made" v. 19; see also Titus 1:1–3; Eph. 1:3, 7, 11–14). Every doctrine of Christian theology is elemental to the covenant and coheres with the entire body of

Christian truth only by means of the unifying reality of the Trinity. The covenant operates in the framework of Trinitarian theology and confirms a soteriological witness to the doctrine of the Trinity (4:4, 6–7; 5:24–25).

Recent Titles from Free Grace Press

The Gospel Made Clear to Children
Jennifer Adams

Beautifully illustrated with short chapters, *The Gospel Made Clear to Children* details the person and work of Christ. It begins with the holiness of God, the sinfulness of man, and the penalty for sin. It considers the love of God in eternity past and the provision God has made in sending His Son. It traces the incarnation, birth, life, and ministry of Jesus Christ, with a special focus on His crucifixion, resurrection, ascension, and exaltation. It culminates with a call to repent and believe, ending with the evidence of true conversion. Written from a heart full of love, this book calls children to turn from their sins and trust in Christ.

The Gospel Made Clear to Children Study Guide
Jennifer Adams

The Gospel Made Clear to Children Study Guide is to be used alongside *The Gospel Made Clear to Children* book. This companion guide takes a deeper look into the Scripture verses mentioned in the book. The study questions promote reflection and application, moving truth from the head to the heart. The goal is to help children be not only hearers of the Word but also doers. Each section ends with a brief prayer, encouraging children to ask the Lord for grace and help.

> "The highest recommendation I can give to this wonderful book is that I will be reading it over and over again to my children. It is rich in biblical doctrine and is an invaluable instrument to aid parents in teaching their children the glorious truths of "God in Christ" reconciling the world to Himself. I know of no other book that so clearly communicates the great doctrines of the gospel to children."

> – *Paul Washer,*
> *Author, Director of HeartCry Missionary Society*

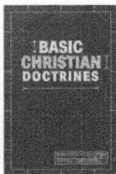

Basic Christian Doctrines
Dr. Curt Daniel

Basic Christian Doctrines is very much what the title suggests—a concise introduction to the fundamental doctrines taught in the Bible. In fifty short chapters consisting of ten simple points each, Daniel presents a thorough introduction to evangelical Christian theology. Those who want a short and non-technical summary of basic Christian theology will find this an excellent tool for Sunday school classes, home Bible studies, homeschools and Christian high schools, and personal Bible study. *Basic Christian Doctrines* is an important, useful handbook every Christian should keep close at hand.

"Usually, other attempts to accomplish a work like this fall flat. Either the subjects are treated with far too much verbiage—thus unnecessarily lengthening the prose, or else easy enough to read but are much too elementary in content. Daniel, however, deftly succeeds with both aims where many other writers do not."

– *Dr. Lance Quinn,*
Executive Vice-President, The Expositors Seminary, Jupiter, FL

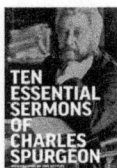

Ten Essential Sermons of Charles Spurgeon
Charles Spurgeon, with an introduction by Tom Nettles

"Charles Haddon Spurgeon had no peer in the theological density of his sermons. At the same time, he had no peer in their simplicity. He looked at truth, to which Christ came to bear witness and embody, as the pathway not only for altering the mind but for shaping the affections. These ten sermons exemplify this pattern of deep doctrine, simple but elegant and engaging presentation, and a call to faith and love. ...The effort to isolate ten influential sermons from a preacher who preached thousands of such sermons is daunting. These sermons, however, succeed in illustrating Spurgeon's doctrine, his evangelistic commitment, the beauty of his language, the manner in which a biblical text suggests a subject, and his passion for the glory of the triune God and the eternal well-being of souls."

– *from the introduction by Tom Nettles*

The Missionary Crisis: Five Dangers Plaguing Missions and How the Church Can Be the Solution
Paul Snider, foreword by Paul Washer

The Missionary Crisis confronts five dangers facing missionaries and the local churches that send them and gives biblical and practical instruction for missionaries, sending churches, and mission organizations. This book boldly approaches gentle correction for the missionary to reverse these five crises in their ministries. It challenges the local church to prepare and equip men and women for the high calling of missionary life.

> "Paul Snider's book, *The Missionary Crisis*, is like looking through a window. He divulges the plight of modern missions with engaging reality. As a missionary, Paul's perspective will afford the reader a much greater concern for what is called today kingdom advancement. Years ago, a mission director said that "the mission field is littered with uncrucified flesh." His assessment, both then and now, is accurate. But Paul doesn't stop after exposing the encumbrances to global missions; he offers biblical and practical solutions to the problems. Local churches, mission agencies, and anyone with an interest in gospel mission enterprise will profit immensely from this superb work."

> *– Don Currin, HeartCry Missionary Society*
> *Eastern European Coordinator*

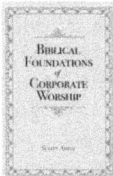

Biblical Foundations of Corporate Worship
Scott Aniol

Ever since Cain and Abel, God's people have been asking, "What is the proper way to worship God?" In five compelling chapters, Scott Aniol explains that corporate worship theology and practice must be founded in the Word of God. There, we discover that corporate worship's goal is communion with God through regular, weekly covenant renewal, wherein the entire congregation engages in dialogue with God in a meeting structured around the gospel, toward the goal of spiritual fellowship with God through Christ by the Spirit.

"The devilish attack of deformation transcends beyond the doctrines of Scripture to the functionality of the church. The church and Scripture are inextricably bound together. Therefore, the need of the hour is biblical reformation of the church's worship. Scott Aniol does an excellent job of directing our attention to Scripture and warning us of the steady stream of man-centered worship philosophies that are constantly luring Christians outside the boundaries of Scripture."

—*Josh Buice, Pastor, Pray's Mill Baptist Church, Douglasville, GA, President, G3 Ministries*

The Failure of Natural Theology: A Critical Appraisal of the Philosophical Theology of Thomas Aquinas
Jeffrey D. Johnson

"Johnson's scholarly but gracefully readable text shows that his intellect notwithstanding, Aquinas's mingled metaphysics, mixed methodology, and promotion of "divine immobility" merit strong caution. This is the book the church has needed on this subject. It is an urgent read by one of our best theologians."

—*Dr. Owen Strachan*

"Jeff's book is a welcome contribution to the debate that is and should be going on in Reformed circles about the value of Thomism in general and the usefulness of his natural theology in particular."

—*Dr. Sam Waldron*

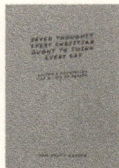

Seven Thoughts Every Christian Ought to Think Every Day: Laying a Foundation for a Life of Prayer
Jim Scott Orrick

In *Seven Thoughts Every Christian Ought to Think Every Day*, Jim Scott Orrick examines the seven thoughts that lead Christians to pray guided by the model prayer. You might think of this book as a prequel to the Lord's Prayer. Without the underlying thoughts of a renewed nature, simply repeating the Lord's Prayer becomes an instance of the empty, meaningless prayers that Jesus was teaching us to avoid. Orrick explores the seven thoughts that propel a Christian into a life of meaningful communion with God through prayer. These are seven thoughts every Christian ought to think every day, and they lay a foundation for a life of prayer.

> "Searching for great resources to disciple new believers can be like Goldilocks tasting porridge. Too difficult, and it frustrates; too fluffy, and it misleads. Jim Orrick has that much sought-after gift of taking deep truths and bringing the tray to the common man. When a book can be handed to an unbeliever for evangelism, read through with a new believer to disciple, worked through with the family for worship, and also delight the soul of the seasoned in Christ, it is a helpful book."
>
> – *Josh Lagrange, Church planter*

On Your Heart: A Three-Year Devotional for Families
A.J. Genco

In 2003, inspired by USAF Colonel Rick Husband of the space shuttle Columbia, A. J. Genco set out to write a devotional for his own family, laboring over it for ten years. Yet when he had barely finished, he was taken from this earth by a sudden illness. Though this devotional was never intended for publication, A. J.'s widow desired for it to be published to honor his legacy. Now not only may you and your family be blessed by this resource but we also hope you would be inspired to leave a spiritual legacy for your own family.

This book includes:

- A family devotional based on a three-year cycle through the Bible
- A "Read through the Bible" guide for parents and older children
- Daily "Family Worship" lessons for the whole family
- A psalm or a portion of a psalm to read each Sunday
- Excerpts from the Baptist Confession of Faith and Nicene Creed

Baptist Reprints Series

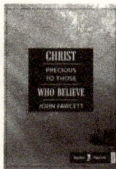

Christ Precious to Those Who Believe
John Fawcett

Written in 1799, *Christ Precious to Those Who Believe* by John Fawcett is a "minor spiritual classic of the eighteenth century that deserves to be better known. In it, Fawcett explores the way that 'love is the parent and promoter of everything excellent and amiable in the Christian character,' a love that is, first and foremost, a love for the Lord Jesus Christ" (adapted from the introductio by Michael Haykin).

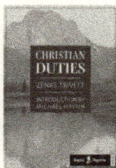

Christian Duties
Zenas Trivett

Christian Duties, originally entitled *Plain Christian Duties Recommended*, is an address Zenas Trivett gave at the establishment of a new Baptist congregation in 1791, in which he lays out the various responsibilities of a faithful member of a local church. Trivett emphasized that congregational polity was "the alone [only] plan of the New Testament," though he urged his hearers never to dream that "all true religion [is] confined to your own denomination." He particularly urged the congregation to often "meet together ... for prayer and conversation," for believers who come together "destitute of the spirit of devotion," Trivett noted, have "their cold affections warmed.".

Visit
www.FreeGracePress.com
for these and many
other excellent resources.

www.ingramcontent.com/pod-product-compliance
Lightning Source LLC
Chambersburg PA
CBHW022010090426
42741CB00007B/965